"Antonio has written an extremely touching relationship between two 18-year-olds, each reluctantly but inexorably drifting into their first gay relationship… writing dialogue that is subtle and sweet, never putting a foot wrong."
—Richard Ouzounian, *Toronto Star*

"What makes *In Gabriel's Kitchen* compelling to watch—aside from marking the promising debut of a new playwright—is the confidence with which Antonio plunders other genres liberally while remaining aware of the limitation of each. In terms of style and content, there are traces of the teen-issue play; the gay coming-out story and the ethnic-family drama, to name but a few. What he has done… is lend them all a more ceremonial, deliberately portentous, dramatic shape. The contemporary genres listed above are distilled through traditions as ancient and as far-flung as Japanese theatre, Greek drama and Christian miracle plays. …A modern tragedy. …There's a determination to look at familiar stories and their theatrical expressions from new angles. …Without turning his play into a diatribe against religious observance or Italian traditional machismo, Antonio offers a message of tolerance and understanding."
—Kamal Al-Solaylee, *The Globe and Mail*

IN GABRIEL'S KITCHEN

In Gabriel's Kitchen

Salvatore Antonio

Playwrights Canada Press
Toronto • Canada

In Gabriel's Kitchen © 2006 Salvatore Antonio
The moral rights of the author are asserted.

Playwrights Canada Press
The Canadian Drama Publisher
215 Spadina Avenue, Suite 230, Toronto, Ontario CANADA M5T 2C7
416-703-0013   fax 416-408-3402
orders@playwrightscanada.com • www.playwrightscanada.com

CAUTION: This play is fully protected under the copyright laws of Canada and all other countries of The Copyright Union, and is subject to royalty. Changes to the script are expressly forbidden without the prior written permission of the author. Rights to produce, film, or record, in whole or in part, in any medium or any language, by any group, amateur or professional, are retained by the author, who has the right to grant or refuse permission at the time of the request. For professional or amateur production rights, please contact Playwrights Canada Press at the above address.

No part of this book, covered by the copyright hereon, may be reproduced or used in any form or by any means—graphic, electronic or mechanical—without the prior written permission of the publisher except for excerpts in a review. Any request for photocopying, recording, taping or information storage and retrieval systems of any part of this book shall be directed in writing to Access Copyright, 1 Yonge Street, Suite 800, Toronto, Ontario CANADA M5E 1E5   416-868-1620.

Financial support provided by the taxpayers of Canada and Ontario through the Canada Council for the Arts and the Department of Canadian Heritage through the Book Publishing Industry Development Programme, and the Ontario Arts Council.

 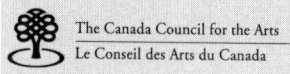 

Front cover photo by Trevor Haldenby
Cover design: JLArt with Salvatore Antonio
Production Editor: Michael Petrasek

Library and Archives Canada Cataloguing in Publication

Antonio, Salvatore
    In Gabriel's kitchen / Salvatore Antonio.

A play.
ISBN 978-0-88754-670-9

1. Suicide--Drama. I. Title.

PS8601.N86I5 2007   C812'.6   C2007-900958-1

First edition: April 2007.
Printed and bound by Canadian Printco Ltd. at Scarborough, Canada.

For A.B.
Dedicated to the spirit of S.M.

"When there is nothing left to burn,
you have to set yourself on fire." —Stars

Table of Contents

Acknowledgements	iii
Introduction by David Oiye	v
Playwright's Notes	ix
Notes on Pace, Punctuation and Grammar	xi
Characters	xv
Setting	xvii
Production Information	1
In Gabriel's Kitchen	3
"The Angel Gabriel" (Gabriel's Message) Music	107
Author's Biography	108

Acknowledgements

In Gabriel's Kitchen was nine years in the writing, from its beginning as a 15-page playwriting assignment, while I was an acting student at the National Theatre School in Montreal, to the final workshop of the 160-page, over full-length script at Buddies In Bad Times Theatre, in Toronto. Along the way, many people have championed this story, and supported me as a writer in various capacities: actors, playwrights, teachers, mentors, audience members, family and friends. The list of people to thank by name has grown to an overwhelming length—I am grateful to all the artists and friends who read the play, who participated in early readings and workshops of the script, who helped me craft this story into a play—the insight you all offered proved invaluable to me in this process. For encouragement, support, and guidance—I am indebted to the following people: Damien Atkins, Molly Atkinson, Marc Bendavid, Kym Bird, Felicia Migliore-Brennan, Diane D'Aquila, Arleen Glickman, Ellen-Ray Hennessey, David Oiye, Sheldon Rosen, Edward Roy, and Judith Thompson.

Special thanks to my classmates from the National Theatre School of Canada, for breathing the first breath into the idea, and to the 2002/2003 Antechamber Writer's Unit at Buddies In Bad Times for helping me develop the full script.

I must also thank Arkady Spivak (Artistic Director, Talk Is Free Theatre) for organizing a public staged reading of this latest revision of *In Gabriel's Kitchen*, in September 2006. The reading was directed by Maja Ardal, with the following actors: Jordan Bell, Eric Craig, Maria Ricossa, Steve Ross, and Justin Stadnyk.

Extra special thanks to the entire creative and technical team of the Buddies In Bad Times premiere production, for their patience and courage. And to the brave and noble cast of the premiere production; I am deeply grateful for your generosity of spirit, and most importantly—your trust.

Introduction

Working with Salvatore as a director and dramaturge is like climbing into the car of a rickety rollercoaster. You know it's dangerous, you feel you shouldn't do it, but everything in your body says that you want to do it and once the ride is over, you have the illogical desire to do it all again.

Salvatore writes passionately. Word.

When I first read that early draft of *In Gabriel's Kitchen* it was essentially a handful of scenes around a kitchen confrontation. I was captivated by the emotion and the urgency of these characters. I could feel the pain and sadness, the anger and the pride. And I could smell the pasta steaming on the table, ignored by the characters too intent on trying to hurt each other into being honest.

For Salvatore, these characters are real... so real that he felt compelled to empty his closet to find clothing that was "exactly right" for the suburban Italian-Canadian kid, a habit that drove our costume designer to threaten violence. (I remember Salvatore calmly explaining that the "hoodie was nice, but, an Italian mother like Concetta, would never let her son wear that sweater because the hood recalls monks and monasteries and an unwed life for her youngest son.")

Every detail was etched so clearly in his mind, from the music which played as an underscoring *leitmotif* for each character, to the lighting effects and set design which would create his universe. It was sometimes a little victory if something which arose out of our rehearsals made it into the script. We would work a piece of movement or staging and if Salvatore liked it, when he did the next sweep of the draft, there it would be. Right alongside the outlandish theatrical devices that we attempted (I cajoled our lighting designer into giving us a semblance of the "cathedral of light") and those which I judiciously chose not to use; the footlights "with brushed-gold shell backings" have yet to be given their stage run. To his credit, Salvatore did allow for a certain amount of compromise when it came to interpreting his vision of the "world of the play"—he would, however defend other elements (i.e: falling dough and rolling styrofoam planets) by asking that an attempt at them be made first, before conceding. The world of this play is unlike most family dramas that you're likely to encounter. Straddling somewhere between kitchen sink and tragic opera, the play constantly surprises with its grand vistas and detailed moments of quiet. This juxtaposition is what strikes home as truly naturalistic—and poetic. There are moments of heightened drama and quiet desperation in every day.

Creating theatre is not just about writing a plot which supports the arc of the story or developing characters with depth and conflict. It is about bringing to life a world which, for the few short hours of each performance, can completely envelop the audience, draw them in, and send them out again with a slightly changed perspective on their lives, and on the world around them. As a director, I often find myself watching the audience more than the play, and regularly, I was surprised at the constant nodding of recognition I would see throughout the audience, at a comment or a response one character would have for another. The audience talkbacks were filled with people exclaiming "I know exactly who Concetta is" or "Paolo reminded me so much of my father." All throughout the play's workshops and rehearsals, our various casts constantly offered up anecdotes, comparisons and reminiscences of family idiosyncrasies from every cultural background imaginable.

The connection that the audience invariably feels with the play is no coincidence. We all have family, right? During a discussion of *In Gabriel's Kitchen*, someone asked (and they were not alone in their sentiments), "aren't the politics of the play dating it a little? Haven't we covered the whole 'struggle of coming out' over the past quarter-century? Look around at the media, film, theatre, politics. They all speak to a more enlightened view of tolerance." Salvatore responded that this was no doubt the case, but that his intent was to take the whole question back into the family unit. While we wear our political progress on our sleeve, how many of us wear an entirely different persona around those nearest and dearest to us?

Perhaps the canvas of the play is not so dated after all. I know half a dozen Gabriels in my circle alone, from different age groups and social circles, different nationalities and occupations. Fear of upsetting those we love is a great motivator. The characters of the Montesano clan are trapped. Trapped by their passion, their traditions and their pride. But most importantly, by their love. Paolo and Concetta are neither evil nor good. They are simply human in the most flawed way. Marco's pain at all the things he is incapable of—comforting his brother, freeing his parents, setting the course of his own life back on track—is palpable and terrible. Matt, alone, with the clarity of an outsider, seems able to grope towards a sense of understanding, and if this speaks of a hint too much clarity, well chalk it up to the brash bravado of youthful optimism—both Matt's, and Salvatore's.

But if there is youth in his writing, there is something more parental in his process. Salvatore will always be the ultimate show mother, the Italian Mama Rose, who sits in the audience of his work, nodding his head emphatically to the beats, mouthing every word and sitting on his hands to keep from openly gesticulating pace and tempo (something I forced him to do whenever he came to rehearsals).

I believe the rehearsal process for this play was even more difficult for Salvatore than for any of us actually in the room. A playwright's work is like his child and a first play is often the most precious and difficult to let go of. During our rehearsals for *In Gabriel's Kitchen*, Salvatore (also a popular actor) was rehearsing as a cast member, in another play in Toronto, a tense emotional drama in which he played the title role. As an absentee father, he did very well, popping in at the end of his rehearsals to see how our day went and to see if there were any questions. How painful it must be for a parent to watch his child grow up and develop characteristics, traits and choices far from what they had imagined at conception. How similar is the relationship a playwright has with his work—full of the same joyful triumphs and proud moments, but equally rife with sad partings and tearful misgivings.

And so, with this book, I watch Salvatore do one of the most painful things possible—send his child out into the world unattended, save for this brief introduction to the two of them.

David Oiye
December, 2006

Playwrights Notes

In Gabriel's Kitchen was written specifically for the theatre. This play was designed to be performed, rather than read as a literary piece—so that much of what may seem obtuse on the page, can only make sense in the execution of the scene. First and foremost, I am an actor; much of what appeared on the pages of my early drafts read like transcribed performance from inside my head. In reviewing these "transcripts," quite often I was surprised by what my characters would say and do; there was very little conscious planning in terms of where a character was going to end up—or more importantly, what they were capable of. Dramatic structure was something I would work on in later drafts. If I had to describe the style of writing in this play, I would say it is poetic naturalism. For the most part, the dialogue is naturalistic. The characters, situations, emotions, are all real. The world in which the story plays out on stage, is one where anything is possible; visitations, the conjuring of the departed or the holy, fantastic understandings, spiritual transportation, and unbridled personal truths. The juxtaposition of the very nature of flesh-and-blood human beings, in a world with changeable realities, created accidental poetry.

The story is essentially about love and loss, in all their forms. I wanted to explore the inherent theatricality of human beings navigating their way through major endings and beginnings, but whom, in the end, are trying to reconcile themselves to life. Despite the unmistakable tragedy of *In Gabriel's Kitchen*, this play is actually a fierce celebration of life—and most importantly the ownership of one's own life. There is much joy and light built into the fabric of the story. The scenes where the family was intact, or where first-love is being discovered are meant to hum with life and humour, without any trace of the known outcome. We will only care about the survivors, if we get to experience who they were before the devastation. The play in performance must earn it's ending; and this play is meant to end with hope… above all else, hope.

Salvatore Antonio
January, 2007

Notes on Pace, Punctuation and Grammar

The stage directions, such as they are, were written by the author and are part of the text. They should be noted not so much as direction for the actors but as intention of the characters.

The idiosyncratic use of grammar and punctuation adheres directly to author's intent—and should be followed in order to achieve the character's specific rhythm, and the designed pace of the play.

The pace within the dialogues and speeches of these characters is very specific—and has been written into the lines using my punctuation—albeit idiosyncratic. The most important thing to understand is that these people speak, for the most part, without thinking first. They figure out what they're trying to say as they're saying it. Emotion, and need, is the motor behind what these characters are saying—rather than an enjoyment of audience. Without the text moving at a real clip, this play has been shown time and again, to deteriorate into melodrama and preciousness—which is not what I intended. When the punctuation is respected the writing allows for the characters to reveal their "true" selves quite often by "accident."

Along with pace, I try to stay true to the "world picture" or education of the characters by respecting certain uses or misuses of grammar.

My use of punctuation or *lack* thereof, is intentional. It speaks to the emotional state of the character. I will attempt to clarify what the punctuation means in this script—acknowledging that this is *not* the universally accepted usage.

When ellipses [...] occur in this script it is almost like the character has lost steam on a particular thought, and is drifting onto a conclusion, or clarification.

When an em-dash [word—word] separates text within the body of dialogue, it is making a solid and definite link to the thought that follows. It can also mean a jump to clarifying what preceded the punctuation. Usually an em-dash appears to show the character condensing their point into a clear statement.

When an em-dash [dialogue section—] appears at the end of a section of dialogue it means the character following them, will abruptly interrupt that line. Therefore the actor also needs to pay attention to the punctuation that precedes their own line.

When an en-dash [–] appears before a line it means that character is not being given full audience by the character they're speaking to. Therefore the line may have to overlap the others dialogue.

When a slash [/] appears in the script it means the character that follows in the text will begin speaking their line at that spot until they reach a full stop within their own text. The lines will overlap. Sometimes two or more slashes will appear within a certain section which is a sign that the pace of the scene is quite rapid, and the emotional investment is high.

When a colon [:] appears in the script, it usually means that whatever follows it is being used to clarify what preceded it using a more cerebral or logical line of thought, i.e. the brain.

When a semi-colon [;] appears in the script, it usually means the clarifying line of thought is more emotional, i.e. the heart.

When a single word is [*italicized*], it usually means that the word has been carefully, or specifically arrived at to explain, clarify or stress. Non-English words not in common usage are also italicized.

When a *single* word is CAPITALIZED, it is usually an explosive point in an already heated argument. It is usually tactical; used in an attempt to stop the other person's argument, or to regain attention or order.

When an entire *line*, or section of text is CAPITALIZED, it is usually being delivered at a high intensity, in order to drive home a point that is being ignored, or skirted around.

When a *(beat)* occurs in the script, it is a momentary shift in the characters argument, or tactic, or awareness. A *(beat)* is not meant to last longer than a quick inhalation, at most.

When a *(pause)* occurs in the script, it usually means that whatever has preceded the pause has derailed the character in some way, and the pause allows for a brief moment to regroup or prepare for what follows it. If it helps to think in terms of breath, an inhalation and exhalation.

When a *(silence)* occurs in the script it is usually a shared non-verbal scene, where a certain truth has been revealed, or a certain belief has been destroyed. A *(silence)* is the most uncomfortable, terrifying shift that can occur in this script. It has an element of danger to it, in that no thing and no one, is safe. A *(silence)* lasts for one beat after the height of discomfort has been reached.

S.A.

Phonetic Pronunciation of Names & Words

Montesano … Monte<u>sah</u>noh
Marco … <u>Mahr</u>rcoh
Concetta … Kohn<u>chet</u>tah
Gabriel … <u>Gay</u>breel
Gabriele (Italian pronunciation) … Gahbree<u>yay</u>lay
Paolo … <u>Pah</u>ohloh
Raphaele (Italian pronunciation) … Rahfa<u>yay</u>lay

Ascoltami (Italian: "listen to me") … Ahs<u>kohl</u>tahmee
Pasta … <u>Pah</u>stah
Grazie (Italian: "thank you") … <u>Grrah</u>tsyay
Mille (Italian: "a thousand") … <u>Mee</u>lay
Pazzo (Italian: "crazy") … <u>Pah</u>tsoh

Text Substitutions

Scene Thirteen: In the event that the actor playing Concetta can not learn the Italian prayer, the English translation may be used in its place.

Scene Seventeen: In the event that the play is being produced in a geographical location where "Woodbridge" is not known as a reference to a wealthy Italian suburb, the following line substitutions may be used:

GABRIEL	I was just fooling around, you know. I was imitating our aunt Carmela from last night. You know how she's all…

> *He mimes a prissy woman fussing with her hands and hair.*

	Mink coat.
MARCO	Mink coat? That's it?
GABRIEL	That's all you need to describe her. Mink coat. 'Nuff said.

> *They laugh.*

Continue on as scripted.

The Christmas carol, "Gabriel's Message," was translated into English by Sabine Baring-Gould, 1834–1924.

Characters

MARCO Montesano: Late twenties. First-generation Italo-Canadian. The lone-surviving son in the family. Very much his father's son—he is a hard worker, who is not comfortable with his emotions. A major part of him died with his brother, and he is desperately trying to redefine himself. A troubled young man, trying to move forward.

CONCETTA Montesano: Mid- to late forties. Italian. Mother to Marco and Gabriel. Wife to Paolo. Once a strong, warm woman, in the "Anna Magnani" tradition—she has been shattered by the suicide of her youngest son. She flounders through the banalities of living. A lonely housewife, in the most severe and manic grips of denial and sadness—although she appears outwardly "fine." She operates in several versions of reality.

GABRIEL Montesano: Late teens. First-generation Italo-Canadian. The youngest son in the family. The "golden boy." Intelligent and sensitive. His blessings and his curse are his artist's eyes, and his poet's mouth. A young man, trying to come to terms with the ramifications of his blossoming sexuality.

PAOLO Montesano: Late forties to early fifties. Italian. Father to Marco and Gabriel. Husband to Concetta. Raised in an "Old World" model of living. He attempted to temper the rigidity of the "old way," with a slightly more liberal approach to raising his family. He blames himself for the disintegration of his family, and now lives a sad, disconnected existence.

MATTHEW (MATT) Finnerty: Late teens. A Canadian kid of Scottish/Irish background. A quick-witted free spirit. Into skateboarding and reading Jack Kerouac. The kind of teenager who can't wait to be in his mid-twenties, he drinks black coffee and smokes strong cigarettes. He comes from a stereotypical uninspiring home life; his working-class parents remain unhappy in an expired relationship. He rejects boundaries, and is allowing himself to fully explore his attraction to Gabriel. This will likely end up being his only homosexual experience.

Setting

Locations: A middle-class suburban house. A deck arch bridge carrying four lanes of traffic over a valley in a major city (based on the Prince Edward Viaduct in Toronto, Canada).

Time: The main storyline involving MARCO and CONCETTA takes place in the present. The second storyline involving GABRIEL and MATT and the active family, takes place three years earlier. PAOLO's solo scenes exist in a chronological "vacuum." The play's narrative continually switches back and forth between past and present.

Place: The actual set should be more of a "frame" of the playing space—a clear periphery in which the story can be told. The playing space should take up as much of the stage as possible, in order to suggest the dimensions of the unfinished basement of a house. Most importantly, it is an unfinished space: incomplete. Plastic sheet wrap, insulation, uncovered sockets, dust in the air. Everything suggests the eeriness of a space abandoned mid-construction. Poured-concrete floors. No doorways. The walls should be of a low height, to further give the feel of a basement. The "walls" themselves are simply suggested by untreated 2x4 lumber frames—it is vital the actors be able to see, and walk through most parts of them. Electrical wires and switches snake through the frames like a network of veins. Hundreds of naked 100-watt bulbs are suspended by wires, above the space, at varying heights, almost creating a "cathedral of light." The lights will glow at varying intensities throughout the story, in order to indicate changes in time and focus. A huge wooden beam rests by one end, on top of the rear wall and continues through the playing space, off the apron of the stage, and into the air through the audience—connecting to the structure. The wood of this one dominant beam should glow brighter than any of the other lumber. It is where Gabriel tied his rope. A huge wood kitchen dining table dominates the stage. It is exaggeratedly large, almost running the width of the stage—it will serve as a secondary playing space, and so should be able to carry the weight of the entire cast. Four simple wood chairs are placed away from the table, facing the would-be walls—they will be positioned at the table for Scene Three. Through the openness of the walls of the playing space, the light, spilling out, catches domestic debris and remnants; the sad ruins of an emptied family life: hundreds of broken plates, empty picture frames, donation bags of clothing, broken mirrors, etc. Everything seems blanched of colour by the elements—faded almost to white. What set details and props are used to suggest the kitchen, depend on the design—however, minimalism is key to the tone of the piece, and will help facilitate the jumps in time and "reality." Props handled by actors should always be real i.e.; steaming plate of pasta, duffel bag, dough.

In Gabriel's Kitchen was first produced at Buddies In Bad Times Theatre in Toronto, Canada, in March 2006, with the following company:

MARCO	Paul Fauteux
CONCETTA	Toni Ellwand
GABRIEL	Marc Bendavid
MATT	Kristopher Turner
PAOLO	Michael Miranda

Director: David Oiye
Dramaturge: Edward Roy
Set and Costume Design: Dennis Horn
Lighting Design: Jeff Logue
Original Music & Sound Design: Marc Desormeaux
Stage Manager: Amber Archbell
Assistant Director: Chris Reynolds
Production Assistant: Rachel Cassidy-Cree

In Gabriel's Kitchen was subsequently produced in Italian, with a revised text, at Teatro Della Limonaia in Florence, Italy, in October 2006, with the following company:

MARCO	Lorenzo Guagni
CONCETTA	Carmen di Bello
GABRIEL	Michele Bellini
MATT	Iacopo Reggioli
PAOLO	Roberto Gioffrè

Translated into Italian by: Pietro Bontempo
Director: Michele Panella

This published text is a revised version of the production script, that includes sections rewritten since the Buddies In Bad Times premiere.

(l to r:) Michael A. Miranda, Toni Ellwand, Marc Bendavid, Paul Fauteux, Buddies in Bad Times production, March, 2006.
photo by Dennis Horn

IN GABRIEL'S KITCHEN
ACT I
Pre-show

The set should stand naked in the theatre's worklights, so that every detail is unapologetically displayed. The apron of the stage is lined by footlights with brushed-gold shell backings (in the old theatrical tradition)—this refined production element should contrast the apparent lack of tech on the rest of the stage. The sound of cold wind surrounds and encircles the theatre, as if the set were in the centre of a circular wind-tunnel. At the ten-minute call, the technical elements of the production begin to layer themselves onto the stage, i.e.: work-lights off, certain lights warm. The theatrical 'state' is slowly built in front of the audience. Until we are left with:

Scene One

Darkness. Cold wind, then: The sound of feedback begins to build a wall of sound; terrible and beautiful, familiar and foreign. Backlights slowly rise to reveal the silhouettes of PAOLO, MARCO, GABRIEL and CONCETTA. They stand on the kitchen table, facing out to the audience. Footlights slowly rise to fill in their forms. They exhale all their breath. They stand in almost religiously neutral poses. Their faces, however, portray no clear expression; almost a vacuum of emotion. A fierce emptiness. In unison they slowly, almost imperceptibly lean their weight forward, they take staggered inhalations as they continue leaning until they risk losing their balance. Freeze. The wall of sound has stripped away, leaving only the sound of feedback. GABRIEL loses his balance, falls forward a step, and quickly flails back, hands in air, falling onto his back. The feedback disappears, leaving only the intense strains of a cello as the lights snap to black.

In darkness, the most human-sounding instrument—the cello; like the voice of a guide, changes in quality to link us to the next scene, the next period in time.

Scene Two

MATT stands at the front of a class. There is a sombre feel to the way he is dressed, although still very much a teenager with a hipster, street sense to his style: dark jeans and dark long-sleeved shirt under a T-shirt. He is in the middle of his presentation on Gravity and the Universe. A model of the solar system is set up before him on a desk. He is grief-stricken—trying to regain his composure. He is subdued. He refers to a paper. There is an empty chair that stands out in his would-be class audience.

MATT (*trying to hold back tears*) …I'm sorry …sorry guys. This is uh, a lot harder than I thought it was going to be… but… I need to…

MATT lets out an exhale.

I just. I have to …look, this project taught me a lot—I learned something really important—so it's important for me to complete it. *(beat)* I need to finish this, so—

MATT clears his throat. He is trying to be strong through his obvious broken heart. He reads GABRIEL's words.

…so, "to conclude; Newton's theory of gravity, was that all objects fall to Earth with the same acceleration regardless of mass. At the Earth's surface this is 9.806 metres per second, per second. 'Gravitation,' refers to the attraction between each particle of matter and every other. *(beat)* It is gravity that is constantly pulling our bodies towards the centre of the Earth." *(beat)* So, that's it. That's the end of our—of my presentation…. Um, that's as far as we got. *(beat)* Actually, no… that's not the end. I'm not done yet.

Lights shift.

Scene Three

It is very late in the night. MARCO and PAOLO sit at the kitchen table. It is the night before MARCO is set to fly back to his home in Vancouver.

PAOLO *(muted)* And how is work?

MARCO It's okay. You know, the same old story. *(beat)* It's pretty busy right now. Lots of orders coming in from the States, so… yeah. Very, very busy. So… *(beat)* That's why I'm going back so soon this time—

PAOLO I know.

MARCO I figured I could get some good overtime, you know… the time-and-a-half should make me some good money.

PAOLO I understand, Marco. Don't worry. You do what you need to.

MARCO What about you, Pa?

PAOLO What about me?

MARCO *(beat)* How is everything?

PAOLO looks at him expressionless.

(beat) I mean, with work.

PAOLO What can I tell you: work is work. This one is a long winter. *(beat)* Very long. Colder than normal—people need a good parka. The distributor says the demand is up, so we make more coats than usual.

MARCO That's good. So, you're busy too, then—that's uh… really… good, Pa.

PAOLO Yes. *(beat)* When does the plane leave tomorrow?

MARCO My flight?

PAOLO Yes.

MARCO	Tomorrow afternoon—4:30. It lands at seven—Vancouver time.
PAOLO	Hm. *(beat)* All right Marco, I am going to go up to sleep now.
MARCO	*(disappointed)* Oh… okay, then.
PAOLO	I will say goodbye now, because I won't see you tomorrow before I go to work.
MARCO	It's okay, I'll wake up.
PAOLO	I go at five in the morning.
MARCO	This is a new thing, going at five.
PAOLO	Yes, but there is no reason for you to get up that early.
MARCO	Oh.
PAOLO	We say goodbye now—It's the same.
MARCO	Well… sure, fine.
PAOLO	*(slightly disconnected)* It was good to see you. So… be good. Keep working hard—It's good for you. So, ah…. We will see each other next year, I hope.
MARCO	Isn't 5 a.m. really early for work? You used to leave at seven.
PAOLO	That was before.
MARCO	Before—right… I see. *(beat)* Pa, what do you do there?—The factory's empty until eight.
PAOLO	Marco. *(beat)* Be safe on your trip home. I'll see you next year.

> *PAOLO kisses him once on each cheek. MARCO pulls him into a hug. It is uncomfortable. MARCO releases him.*

MARCO	Well, I guess… um… take care of yourself.
PAOLO	Goodbye Marco—*ciao*.

> *PAOLO turns to leave, just as he is about to exit the space—*

MARCO Stop… please.

> *PAOLO stops and speaks without turning.*

PAOLO What, Marco.

MARCO I just …Look at me, Pa.

> *PAOLO turns.*

PAOLO What.

MARCO What's happening here? *(beat)* Why is she up there, again?

> *PAOLO lowers his eyes.*

(beat) She's in his room. Why? *(beat)* How long is she going to stay in there?

PAOLO *(pause)* I don't know.

MARCO What is she doing in there?

PAOLO I don't …know. Whatever she needs to.

MARCO How long has she been doing this? Every night? Huh? *(beat)* Pa—every night?!

PAOLO Marco. When she is ready, she will come to bed. It's not a problem for you.

MARCO It's not a problem—Are you serious?

PAOLO Get onto your plane tomorrow, have a safe trip, and don't worry about these things.

> *He turns to leave.*

MARCO How am I not supposed to worry? You tell me how I'm not—Pa—

> *MARCO turns PAOLO around by the shoulder, who is in turn, instantly inflated with rage. PAOLO turns and gets right in his face. His hand raised.*

	Pa?! *Easy*, okay!—This is not good for her. *(beat)* I worry for both of you, Pa— / I think we all need to—
PAOLO	/ KEEP your voice down.

> PAOLO *instantly lowers his hand and snaps back into control.*

Marco, *ascoltami*—I am only say this once; leave this alone. No good can come from your questions. Stay quiet, go back to your new home—and be grateful for it.

> PAOLO *holds on his son's eyes for a moment and abruptly leaves.* MARCO *makes his way back to the table and sits. He stares out for a moment, overwhelmed, before putting his head in his arms on the table.*

> Cross into:

Scene Four

> *In a space and lighting state very different than anything up until this point—we meet* GABRIEL *and* MATT. *They are eighteen. Their scene plays out, above the action on stage, as if on a bridge. It takes place three years before the play's beginning. It is late autumn. They have strayed on their way home from school.*

> MATT *holds a skateboard. He wears a marked-up jean-jacket over a zip-up hooded sweatshirt. He wears beat-up Converse high-top All-Stars, and low-riding, punk-tapered jeans.* GABRIEL *is dressed more sensibly, and slightly more conservatively—although still very much a teenager. He is weighed down by both of their knapsacks. They both look over the edge of the railing as if on a high bridge.* MATT *smokes a cigarette.*

MATT	...Dude, I'm telling you, I have no "home." When you're changing your address every couple years, it's almost impossible to use that word; *Home*. We move all the time. So after a while you just start to call it your "house," "the house we live in" ...whatever.
GABRIEL	Wow Matt... that's kinda rough, no?
MATT	Well, there ain't much I can do—cause of my dad's department in the force. They're constantly relocating him—so of course his loser family has to follow wherever he goes. *(beat)* I'm not being a suck about it—it's just, like, a different reality than most people—that's all. *(beat)* Whatever—all I was trying to say before was that, you can live in a house, and still be homeless.
GABRIEL	I guess you're right... I never thought about it that way.
MATT	*(beat)* It's not all that bad. I mean really—I never get a chance to get bored of anything around me, 'cause I know it'll only be there for a year or two before we change houses again. So if something sucks, I'm not stuck with it.
GABRIEL	But what if something's really good? You still have to leave it, right?
MATT	Says who?—Some things you can bring with you, right? *(beat)* Gabriel?
GABRIEL	I guess. *(beat)* You have an answer for everything, don't you?
MATT	I don't know...

They chuckle.

The good thing about moving is that I always get to start over. Almost like I get to be a bit different from the guy I was before. It's like I meet a new group of people—and they don't know me, so I get to like, re-invent myself.

GABRIEL   *(not understanding)* "Re-invent" yourself?

MATT   Well, think about it: You don't know what I was like before I moved here, right? I may have been a big asshole who used to beat people up, or something—you don't know. All you know, is the Matt I've introduced you to. The Matt I am with you.

MATT looks for a response, and realizes GABRIEL isn't on board yet.

Okay, I just met you, what? Like, a few months ago, right?

GABRIEL   Six weeks.

MATT   Six *weeks*? Really?

GABRIEL   Yup.

MATT   Really? Feels like longer.

GABRIEL   I know.

MATT   *(beat)* Anyhow, what was I saying? Right, okay look: I only know the Gabriel that I met. Get it?—The guy who's standing beside me. But if Gabriel had been a, whatever, before I met him, I would be able to find out because everyone knows you here, and they measure who you are now, against the history of who you've been in the past. So, you only have a little room to change or like, experiment, before people pull you back to the version of you they expect. *(beat)* See, people suck, cause it's in our nature to want to change ourselves, but most of us can't accept change in others. I say, fuck that.

GABRIEL   Word.

MATT   Word. See, but I don't need to deal with that shit, because I'm never surrounded by the same people for long. So, if I don't like something about myself—I can change it the next time around without anyone reminding me of what I was—or who I'm supposed to be.

GABRIEL So what, are you, like, an escaped psycho or something?

MATT No, dumbass. I'm talking about all the parts that make up—

GABRIEL I'm kidding! I'm just playing. I understand what you're saying—I do.

MATT Do you? Honestly?

GABRIEL Yes.

MATT Okay good—'cause it's important that you get this about me.

GABRIEL I do. *(beat)* I'm kinda jealous, actually—you're like, never locked into one version of yourself, so you can always try out different parts of who you are—/

MATT That's it. / Exactly.

GABRIEL —Or who you could be… I think that's really cool. You're lucky.

MATT I don't know about "lucky," it's just how I've learned to deal with my situation. Them the breaks, right? It's all about what you do with what you're given, I guess. Bitch and moan, or just get on with it.

GABRIEL Hm. Very cool.

MATT Why thank you, Gabriel.

GABRIEL Well, you're welcome—Matt.

MATT I think we're both kinda lucky—that we met each other, you know. We get each other.

GABRIEL I agree.

> Beat. GABRIEL looks out. GABRIEL takes all of this in, but remains looking out. MATT surveys GABRIEL, with a smile.

MATT …Gabriel…

> Beat. GABRIEL lowers his head, with a little laugh.

What?

GABRIEL Nothing, it's just that you always do that, eh? You use my name.

MATT Do I? *(beat)* Hmn ...*Gabriel*—Yeah, I do.

GABRIEL It doesn't bug me or anything—actually I think it's kinda— ...I just noticed that you do.

MATT I guess I like saying it. *Gabriel*—It's a really nice name.

GABRIEL Really? Well, thanks.

MATT It's a beautiful name. *(indicating the cigarette)* Shit, it's out again.

GABRIEL Are you serious? Hold up—I think I put your lighter in my bag.

> *He struggles to get the backpack and knapsack off his back and shoulders, so he can retrieve the lighter.*

MATT *(finding it a bit funny)* Sorry, dude. It's 'cause we're high up—the wind's doing it, I swear.

GABRIEL *(disabled by the two bags)* These stupid things weigh a ton. Why can't you just leave your biology book in your locker?

MATT Aw shit, Gabe—you're still carrying my bag!—I'm soo sorry, man.

> *GABRIEL struggles to get the bag off, it gets his arm stuck in an awkward position.*

GABRIEL It's cool—just help me... get it... off. It's stuck. The strap.

MATT Okay—here, lemme get it—sorry, here.

> *He lifts up the bags so GABRIEL can figure out how to release his arms. He finally frees himself. They are close.*

GABRIEL Thanks. *(beat)* I'll... uh... what was I supposed to be doing?

MATT I don't remember.

GABRIEL The lighter, right. *(beat)* Where did I put it?

> *They laugh.*

MATT Maybe it's in your pocket.

GABRIEL Yeah—what, like, the bag pocket, you mean…?

MATT No, no. *(beat)* I think your jeans pocket.

GABRIEL *(not understanding, fully)* My jeans pocket… why would I have your lighter in my…?

MATT Yeah, here hold this *(gives him the cigarette)*—Lemme check.

> *He moves closer. GABRIEL clues in and plays along.*

GABRIEL Ohh. I… right… it might be in my pocket.

MATT Front or back?

GABRIEL *(beat)* Um, front, I think.

> *They are face to face. They look at each other, acknowledging their real motive.*

What are you looking at?

MATT You, Gabriel.

> *MATT gently takes GABRIEL's face in his hands.*

GABRIEL Matt, wait—wait, okay. What if someone sees us?

MATT It's okay. Shhh…

GABRIEL Matt…

MATT Gabe, don't worry… we're just a blur to them. *(He kisses GABRIEL.)* We're nothing.

> *He pulls GABRIEL to him and kisses him deeper. After a moment GABRIEL gently pulls away, and turns to face out over the railing. MATT takes this as a cue to try a softer approach. MATT takes GABRIEL's backpack off, and gently turns him to face him again.*

The two boys hover over each others faces for a long time before finally, gently, arriving at each others lips. The kiss is innocent and new, devoid of any groping or experienced contact. We hear the traffic below, as the sound and lights shift time and place.

Cross into:

Scene Five

Sterile lights rise to reveal a suitcase and a gym bag sitting near the wall. It is the day after Scene Three. The day of MARCO's departure. There is a place-setting on the kitchen table.

MARCO can be heard offstage, agitatedly searching for something. His mother, CONCETTA, stands in the centre of the kitchen, quietly. She is dressed in black mourning with a muted apron, and house slippers. She wipes her hands on a dishcloth. She is nervous and reserved—oddly out of place in her own kitchen, for this brief private moment. She seems fixated on the suitcase and gym bag—as if their very presence is a harbinger of abandonment. She has desperately been trying to appear her "former" self with MARCO, during this visit. The result is unconvincing, sad, and uncomfortable to watch. Her façade is quickly deteriorating.

Silence.

CONCETTA *(in his direction)* Why you never said nothing about my new Nativity set? *(beat)* Hah, Marco? How come?

MARCO *(offstage)* I can't hear you.

CONCETTA The brand new Nativity set, Marco—don't pretend you don't see it. *(beat)* It was a lot of work, you know. I was fixing up the manger last week, because I knew you were coming home for the Christmas. *(beat)* Even though you only did come

	for three days only, this year. I still put it up—for you. *(beat)* Did you hear me?
	MARCO pokes his head in.
MARCO	Thank you for the manger… okay? *(beat)* But I did tell you and Pa before, that I was gonna be picking up other people's holiday shifts. For the extra money. So…
CONCETTA	Oh. *(beat)* I don't remember that.
MARCO	What do you mean, you "don't remember?"
CONCETTA	Well, it's all right, Marco. You are a big boy now… you do things how you want to.
MARCO	Ma, look I'm sorry—but three days is all I could take off this year. It's better than nothing. *(beat)* I have to finish getting ready.
	He goes back out to whatever he was doing.
	CONCETTA grabs her stomach, a brief, subtle flash of pain flashes across her face. After a second she exhales and pats her forehead. This is obviously a common occurrence. She speaks through the pain—like a well-trained actor.
CONCETTA	The manger looks different, no? I made it all nice and real-looking for the new set, you know? Real hay, real moss and plastic flowers for the outside— I used the hot glue gun, even. *(beat)* Hey Marco, you wanna know what happened to me? I was right in the middle of working on it—like a slave, and I heard the doorbell go. It was the stupid girl from up the street. *(beat)* Are you there, Marco?
MARCO	*(offstage)* Holy—Yeah, I can hear you.
CONCETTA	Oh. Well, you know that stupid *mangia*-cake girl— the one with all the teeth.
MARCO	*(offstage)* Which one?
CONCETTA	I don't know which one, Marco! Please! Her, she came to my front door with some paper in her

                hand and a big envelope: "Missa Montesano? Missa Montesano"—Mah, who are these people to me?

MARCO   (*offstage*) They're your neighbours. We used to play with them when we were little.

CONCETTA   I don't got no neighbours. So, anyway, I pretended I'm not home—I crawled out of the front room on my hands and knees into the hallway.

MARCO   (*offstage*) Why would you do that?

CONCETTA   What do you mean?—So she could not see me through the window. Those are the type of people who look into windows if you don't answer the door.

MARCO   (*offstage*) I don't get why you don't just answer the door?

CONCETTA   What do I got to answer the door for, Marco? For what? So they can kill me whenever they want to? (*beat*) (*half to herself*) …Answer the door… pff. (*beat*) Why they can't just leave me alone in my own house? Bothering people. I don't have no money for what she's selling. Since when do these people talk to me? Her mother is the same one who used to criticize me when you two were little boys.

    MARCO enters in a flurry. His parka is on.

    (*instant pain*) Why are you wearing your coat in the house—it's not time yet.

MARCO   I'm cold—this house is freezing.

CONCETTA   Oh. I am very hot… but I was over the stove.

MARCO   (*as if he hasn't heard her*) What am I forgetting?

CONCETTA   That girl rang my doorbell, Marco…. Maybe you don't know this, but that girl's mother gave me a speech once, about how it was cruel to give my children Nutella sandwiches. *Cruel.* Pfft! Like she was my queen, or something. My boys were

	happy with their chocolate sandwich. You were happy though, no? See?!
MARCO	*(ignoring the question)* So I think that's everything…
CONCETTA	You didn't grow up with no curves or nothing.

MARCO checks his pockets. Throughout the next passage his frustration escalates far greater and faster than is actually warranted.

MARCO	Shit—the things—Where did I put those goddamn things?
CONCETTA	What are you looking for?
MARCO	The things. The, the, / whatever they're called—
CONCETTA	Ahh? / I don't know what "things" you looking for.
MARCO	/The stupid things for the bags—shit!/
CONCETTA	/Easy *easy*, Marco. Come on./
MARCO	/No Ma! I have to find them, or I'm never gonna get out of this place!

He spots them in the outside pocket of his gym bag.

Never mind, NEVER mind, okay—they're right here—

CONCETTA	You gotta calm down yourself, Marco—
MARCO	—*(reading)* BAGGAGE identification tags.
CONCETTA	—Get so exciting, for what? You gonna give yourself a heart attack for a piece of paper—Godforbid.

She immediately finds two separate pieces of wood to knock on, three times each. He sits at the table, and begins filling out his tags.

MARCO	You don't understand, I'm pushed for time, already… I do have to get back home, you know? I don't want to miss the flight.
CONCETTA	THIS is your home.

> *Silence. Neither acknowledges their last comments.*
> ...Cruel.

MARCO What?

CONCETTA She was the bad mother, that one. "Pamela"—stupid name. Criticizing me for the Nutella, while she was giving her childrens those orange slices wrapped in the plastic?—Cheese?!

MARCO *(without looking up)* –You're still talking about this?

CONCETTA *(oblivious to him)* Look how her childrens turned out, ha?—The one is a wobbly-hipped fox, smoking and leaning into cars, and the youngest ended up with no chest and a mouthful of teeth all crisscross—like a trap! Mah please! Why does she send her daughter to my house for now? You want to know why?—Huh, Marco?

> *She is staring at him, expecting the prompt. He looks up from his tags.*

MARCO *(begrudgingly)* Why Ma? Why does she send her daughter to you?

CONCETTA To burn down my manger! That's why!

> *He closes his eyes.*

MARCO What, do you mean.

CONCETTA I am telling you Marco—no joking. By the time she finally walked away from the front door, I got up and came back into the front room—and Mother of God, the light in the manger was making the hay go on fire!

MARCO I see.

CONCETTA Because, I told you, the hay is real!

MARCO So was the 100-watt bulb you had in there, Ma. *(beat)* I changed it to a 20, by the way.

CONCETTA Who? That's why it's not bright no more. Who told you to touch it?!

MARCO	You do not put a 100-watt bulb in a plywood manger filled with real hay, okay? *(beat)* I mean—didn't Pa say anything?
CONCETTA	*(beat)* He don't say nothing about nothing anymore. *(beat)* You know that.

> *A long uncomfortable pause.*

> I got to go take out the pasta.

> *She exits.*

MARCO	Ma, I don't have time to sit and… ugh.

> *He begrudgingly removes his parka and places it on the back of his chair. He rubs his eyes, as if he has a headache.*

> Why did you have to buy a new holy family set, anyway? What was wrong with the old one. *(beat)* These new figures are too big. *(no response)* They're gigantic. *(beat)* Mary and Joseph are the size of my legs almost. *(no response)* It doesn't look right—they can't even fit in the manger.

> *CONCETTA returns with a plate, a fork and spoon. She looks as though she's been crying. She keeps her eyes low.*

MARCO	*(noticing her shift)* …Ma?
CONCETTA	You don't understand. They need to be big like that—so you can see what is in their faces.
MARCO	What are you talking about?
CONCETTA	Because my set is so big, you can see how scared the Blessed Virgin really is—and how nervous poor Joseph is: because he doesn't know for sure if he's doing the right thing with her.

> *She looks MARCO straight in the eyes.*

> You can see their *faith* on their faces.

MARCO	*(beat)* Oh. *(beat)* I see.

As CONCETTA exits into the kitchen:

CONCETTA The figures are the right size: we got to make the manger bigger next year, that's all.

MARCO *(mostly to her direction)* Yeah—why not. Maybe… we should just… convert the whole front room into a real, live manger—with chickens and a mule, even. We could—I don't know, wrap some sheets around us and play out the parts. That might be a fun thing to do.

CONCETTA returns with a can of Brio and a glass. Unimpressed.

CONCETTA Marco, ENOUGH.

MARCO Is it though?—I don't know. I mean we could do better —we could live it, Ma! We could *be* the holy family; You, and me, and Pa.

CONCETTA stares at him, unflinching.

Seriously, can't you picture it? Then, when people would ring your doorbell, they could look in your front window and you would have the best set-up on the street. Then everything would be good, huh? *(beat)* Why not.

CONCETTA Are you finished?

MARCO I don't know, Ma, am I? Are you?

CONCETTA Just sit. *(beat)* The pasta is ready.

MARCO I told you I don't have time to eat the pasta—I TOLD you.

CONCETTA looks at him for a moment, expressionless. She suddenly turns and walks into the kitchen. MARCO stands, troubled. Unsure about how to proceed.

Cross into:

Scene Six

The lights rise on MATT and GABRIEL on the bridge from the earlier scene. They have finished kissing. They both smoke a cigarette. MATT stands on his skateboard and rolls side to side while he speaks. They both look out.

GABRIEL   Hey, watch you don't roll over onto the highway.

MATT   Shyeah, seriously. *(beat)* Guess what—my dad told me that in a couple of years they're gonna cover this bridge, to stop people from jumping.

GABRIEL   Really?—Cover it, how?

MATT   Not cover, I think they're gonna like, put up a really high fence along the railing or something. I'm not sure what exactly, but they're gonna do something.

GABRIEL   That'll look weird. Don't you think?

MATT   Probably. I say, if they wanna jump, let 'em jump.

GABRIEL   Matt, that's mean…

MATT   Why's that mean? It's their life—It should be their choice. We have no idea what's in their head.

GABRIEL   Yeah, but what about the people in the cars below, when they land?

They both look over the edge imagining the impact.

MATT   True, I didn't think of that. That would be nasty, huh? Splat!

They share a little laugh. GABRIEL notices that MATT is staring at him with a little smile on his face.

GABRIEL   *(Re: MATT's focus and smile)* …What? *(beat)* Why are you looking at me like that?

MATT   *(beat)* Look, we like each other, right?

GABRIEL   What.

MATT I'm just saying. I'm not crazy here? We both like each other?—You know, like more / than just—

GABRIEL / Yeah… I think so.

MATT playfully tackles GABRIEL.

MATT You "think" so, eh funny-guy?

Gives him a peck on the mouth, and then gets back on his skateboard.

GABRIEL Come off that thing—You're taller than me to start with.

MATT gets off, and moves in to stand beside him. Shoulder to shoulder. They look out as they speak.

MATT Better? *(pause)* You know, it's kinda weird kissing another guy.

GABRIEL "Weird?"—Thanks.

MATT Naw, come on—I don't mean it that way. Weird in a cool way.

GABRIEL How's that?

MATT I don't know. It's like, we're the same in so many ways, right? So, we kind of fit together—but differently; our *same-ness* is what makes it different.

GABRIEL I'm not sure I get it.

MATT Maybe I don't either, fully. But who gives a shit? *(beat)* Why do we have to understand it? We feel it right?

GABRIEL Yeah.

MATT So…? I feel good with you—in a new way—that I don't fully understand. But, I'm cool with that. You?

GABRIEL I'm cool. *(beat, playing)* But, nowhere near as cool as you.

MATT *(laughing)* Are you making fun of me?

GABRIEL *(laughing)* Me? Never.

>*MATT lightly play-punches GABRIEL's shoulder, but it ends up being an excuse to stay closer to him. GABRIEL grabs his arm, and slowly brings it down, sliding his hand into his. They stand together holding hands, momentarily rendered shy.*

GABRIEL *(overwhelmed by the hand-holding, at a loss to explain)* This is… so… ah…

>*He lets out a huge suppressed exhale.*

MATT *(playfully enjoying the sound)* Ga-br-iel…

GABRIEL Mm-hm?

MATT So, who did you hang out with, before I moved here?

GABRIEL I don't know… people—Sara, mostly.

MATT Blonde Sara? She's cool. *(beat)* Are you happy that I moved here?

GABRIEL *(playing along)* Yes, Matt I'm soo happy you moved here—Now my life is complete.

MATT Gabriel…

GABRIEL Well, what a dumb question. Yeah, of course I'm happy you're here. Can't you tell?

MATT Good, cause I'm happy you're here, too. *(beat)* With me.

>*A silence.*

GABRIEL Matt, um. You don't have to answer or anything, but—have you ever… *done it* …before?

MATT Done what?

GABRIEL It.

MATT "Done it"—like you mean, sex?

GABRIEL Yeah okay—sex.

MATT Yeah, why?

GABRIEL *(beat)* When did you have it?

MATT Do you mean my first time? Or when was the last time I did it?

GABRIEL Okay—maybe I don't want to know.

MATT Relax. The first time was last year.

GABRIEL Oh.

MATT And the last time was before I moved here. *(beat)* And just so you know, both my first, and the last time were with the same girl: my girlfriend back at our last house.

GABRIEL Oh right—the one in Pefferlaw? *Helen*, right?

MATT *(smiling)* Shut up, you remember her name—it's Hillary, not Helen. Dumbass. *(beat)* What about you?

> GABRIEL *says nothing.*
>
> Gabriel, come on—you can tell me, I don't care.

GABRIEL No.

MATT No what? *(beat)* Oh. Never? *(beat)* Not even with Sara?

GABRIEL No. We're just friends.

MATT *(beat)* Oh. *(beat)* Well, it's okay that you haven't.

GABRIEL *(flat)* Is it.

MATT Totally—I mean, I've never done it, with a guy... before, you know. Ever.

GABRIEL Hm.

MATT Seriously. You're the first guy I've ever even fooled around with, Gabriel. *(beat)* So, it's okay 'cause it's new for both of us.

GABRIEL What is?

MATT Everything, I guess.

> GABRIEL *relaxes a bit. They ponder the possibilities.*

GABRIEL *(almost to himself)* ...Gabriel Montesano and Matthew Finnerty—interesting match.

MATT Yeah, Matt Finnerty doesn't have the same ring, does it?

GABRIEL	Sure it does... *Matthew*.
MATT	Not like "Gabriel," though. *(beat, spoken)* "The angel Gabriel, from heaven came; his wings as drifted snow, his eyes a-flame."
GABRIEL	What is that? A poem?
MATT	It's a Christmas carol, dumbass. *(He sings.) The "an-gel Ga-br-iel / from hea-ven came, / his wings as drif-ted snow, / his eyes a-flame; 'All hail,' said he, 'Thou low-ly mai-den Ma-ry / Most high-ly fa-voured la-dy.' / Glo-o-ri-a.*
GABRIEL	I've never heard it before.
MATT	It's called "Gabriel's Message."
GABRIEL	Really?
MATT	Yeah. Pretty cool, eh?—You have your own song.
GABRIEL	I guess, yeah—but I'm no angel, though.
MATT	Shyeah, I kinda figured that. *(beat)* You're staring—what's in your head?
GABRIEL	I'm just looking at you and thinking... thinking, that smoking is the dumbest thing—ever.
	He grabs the cigarette out of MATT's mouth and runs away. MATT pursues him.
MATT	*(laughing)* Gabe, you dumbass! Give it back!
	Cross into:

Scene Seven

Lights come up on MARCO from his previous scene. CONCETTA stands in front of him with a steaming plate of pasta. She is more visibly struggling with her state.

CONCETTA	Now please, Marco, sit.
	She sets it on his place and holds out his chair. A tense beat.
MARCO	*(carefully)* I don't know how to make you understand—I have to go now.

CONCETTA   Again.

She takes off her apron and sits in her seat.

MARCO   Ma, please—do we have to go through this every time I go back, okay? I have to go back—I have work. That's where I live now, Vancouver. So...

She looks at him as though she hasn't heard a word.

CONCETTA   Did I tell you? I still got the pain.

He sits defeated. She unfurls his napkin.

MARCO   The... pain? Still? The same one from before?

CONCETTA   The same one, yes. But now it feels it feels like I got Drano in my stomach.

MARCO   *Drano.* What—well did you go to the doctor?

CONCETTA   I can't move some days. No cleaning. No nothing.

MARCO   Yeah, but did you see the doctor?

CONCETTA   Your father had to reheat leftover food from the fridge once. He never even said a word: he could see I was dying.

MARCO recognizes the timing of this revelation.

MARCO   Okay—you know what? This is crazy—it's like I'm talking to a four-year-old or something.

CONCETTA   He never says nothing no more, your father: he moves around like a shadow and watches the television, loud.

MARCO increasingly agitated, gets up to continue preparing.

MARCO   Nope, I'm not doing this—you're not a baby, you know the number for the doctor. *(beat)* Thank you for the pasta, but I have no appetite. I'm not hungry—

CONCETTA   —Yes, you are gonna get hungry later on the plane!

MARCO   —I gotta go.

CONCETTA	No!
MARCO	Yes! What? No! No, this isn't a *discussion*, okay—I have a ticket!
CONCETTA	You are so skinny.
MARCO	I am not / *skinny*—
CONCETTA	/ Yes SKINNY!—Skinny like an Ethiope!
MARCO	MA PLEASE!
CONCETTA	MARCO! I MADE YOU PASTA!
MARCO	STOP! *(beat)* Okay, just stop it. What are you doing? I am late—I will be late if I stop to eat this. So stop.

CONCETTA stops. With downcast eyes she launches into a slow burn:

CONCETTA	No. All right, Marco, all right—I am stopped. Concetta always got to be the one to stop. *(beat)* I am going to stop real good for once and for all—you'll all see. A BIG STOP!

She launches into the speech with a speed that becomes almost manic.

MARCO	—Ma-okay, calm down…
CONCETTA	You are not gonna find me here next time if you go like this. I'm gonna pack a bag and leave your father and, and… the house. The house! I don't even care if the dust reaches the ceiling—why should I care? No one even hears me anyway. Now that you're gone from here, no one even talks to me—sometimes I go two whole days without saying a word to no one.
MARCO	–Who?
CONCETTA	No one knows if I'm sick or sad—I could cry forever AND loud, and no one would ask me nothing!

MARCO   MA! WHO!? Who do you keep talking about? You keep saying "No one" as if there's a full house—why? It's just you and Pa, here. There's no one else.

CONCETTA   You are right. You are right, Marco. This house is an empty house! And me, I am an abandoned THING—

MARCO   –I know where this is going— / please don't do this—

CONCETTA   / You think even one of your father's sisters would ever call me on the phone? Nothing. Oh no, they paid their respects when they had to, and now my house has the black mark.

MARCO   Stop.

CONCETTA   NO. No. I am stopping hard now—I am going to go far from this stupid place. I am going to get on the Greyhound that goes all the way to Brooklyn, and I am going to buy the house that my sister lived in—God rest her soul—and all I am going to take is my bag, and THIS:

She holds up a glass bead rosary. MARCO freezes—his eyes locked on the rosary. His breath is stopped by the revelation, without any dramatic overlay in behaviour.

Your poor brother's rosary. This is all I will need, and I will be happy, and I will be able to smile again with the whole of my mouth. You watch!

MARCO finally exhales, as if he has come up through water. He turns away.

Only your poor brother knows respect for me. Only him.

MARCO   Ma.

CONCETTA   What do I even care now?

MARCO   *Knew.*

CONCETTA immediately stiffens. She looks at him hard.

Only my poor brother *knew* respect. *(beat)* Why do you keep speaking about him in the present? When are you gonna stop? What are you doing to yourself?

CONCETTA silently gasps and looks away, as if she's been slapped.

How much did you spend on the new headboard, and the new mattress?

CONCETTA steps away from him and stares at him as if he's an uninvited stranger.

Why would you?—MA answer me.

Pause.

I saw it, okay—There is a new bed in Gabriel's room. It's still wrapped in plastic. It wasn't here last time I came home—It's a brand new bed.

CONCETTA	I don't know what you are saying to me.
MARCO	Why is it here?! Why would you go and buy a new bed for his room, when he's not there to sleep in it? I don't get it, Ma!
CONCETTA	You don't need to "get" it. You need to go now.
MARCO	No, you need to answer me. Someone's gotta explain to me—What about Pa? He's just as bad, isn't he? He just pretends he doesn't see what's happening in here?! Jesus Christ.
CONCETTA	MARCO. Just go, please. Go to your new home and leave us alone.
MARCO	What you're doing is not normal, okay?! Do you understand that? Do you hear me?!—

CONCETTA turns on him fiercely.

CONCETTA	You STOP!!

MARCO —You stop! It's been three years of this crazy shit! You think I haven't seen that his *National Geographic*'s keep coming?—And that you keep piling them up in his room, as if he's going to read them? It's not right.

CONCETTA No, no it's not right what *you* do! Why you went in there for? You got none of your business to go in there—do you hear me?!

MARCO We gotta figure this out right here, today—you and me. 'Cause I am not leaving again with the same GODDAMN lump in my stomach that I get every time I come back here. No more. *This*—this has got to stop!

> CONCETTA *gets up and starts to clear away the pasta.*

CONCETTA Can you go now? PLEASE!

MARCO Ma DON'T pretend you can't hear—

> MARCO *physically tries to sit her down.*

Please stop—you've got to stop with this—

> CONCETTA *slaps him across the face.*

CONCETTA —YOU STOP NOW!! Okay you?! You, don't you EVER talk to me like he is only a, a, a PICTURE. Do you understand? That is my boy, when you talk his name. You hear me? I will—I will break your head if you ever try to end him to me. Okay?! Do NOT.

> CONCETTA *takes the plate and the tablecloth. She makes it to the exit, before turning her head without looking at him.*

(*with an eery instant calm, devoid of anger*) You are free to leave now.

> *She exits.* MARCO *stands shaking from it all. Lights change to shift us to:*

Scene Eight

GABRIEL and MATT, in the unfinished basement. A few weeks after we last saw them. They have just come in from the early winter cold—their shoes off, but jackets still on. The room is dark, save for some light spilling in from the basement foyer. MATT stands in the centre of the room, holding a huge contraption wrapped in plastic garbage bags and masking tape. GABRIEL is offstage—we can hear him fumbling to find a light switch. He's dropping papers from the folder he clutches.

GABRIEL Stupid thing. Shit—sorry. I think this is it, right… here.

In the half-light, MATT's contraption tips a bit—sending a white Styrofoam ball rolling across the cement floor.

MATT Ohhp!—there goes another one.

GABRIEL Which one's that?

MATT I think it's one of Saturn's moons.

As MATT goes to put down the project—a few more moons and planets spill out all over the floor.

Aw shit! Are they still labelled?

GABRIEL No worries—we'll figure it out. Ugh, sorry. Just… one… sec—

Finally the lights come up to reveal the two young men, barely holding on to their respective bundles. They laugh at the sight of each other. GABRIEL relieves him of the wire contraption.

MATT Check us out, eh? We're such losers.

They proceed to put down their loads and remove their jackets. GABRIEL is obviously nervous about having MATT at his place for the first time.

GABRIEL Seriously—total losers. Ho-ly, I'm sweating—Can I get you something? Water? Coke?

MATT   I'm okay.

GABRIEL   A chair! I'm retarded—I'll get us chairs—

MATT   It's cool, don't worry about it Gabe. / Gabriel chill.

GABRIEL   / Sorry, this is so ghetto.

MATT   Just relax, it's no big deal—let's just sit on the floor.

GABRIEL   Sorry this is such a dive—my father hasn't really finished it yet.

MATT   Oh. What do you mean "finish?" What's it gonna be?

GABRIEL   Well, it'll look better, like the upstairs kinda—see, this is still the rough-in.

MATT   "Rough-in?" What does that mean?

GABRIEL   The basement hasn't been finished: so right now it's the same as when the house was built. There's nothing here.

MATT   Dude, it's a basement.

GABRIEL   *Dude,* I know that. But when my father decides to, we're going to make it nice and finished. This section over here will probably end up being like a, well—I'm not sure—just like a room or something.

MATT   *(finding this cute)* "Or something?"

GABRIEL   Yeah, but this over here will definitely be a kitchen.

MATT   *(playing with him)* You're sure about that? How do you know?

GABRIEL   *(catching on)* Because, of this... smartass.

> *He indicates a black plastic pipe sticking up through the cement floor. MATT moves in to see.*

MATT   Ohh I see. That's for the—

MATT & GABRIEL   Kitchen sink. / The kitchen sink, yup.

They continue speaking as they move the project materials and their coats into some configuration on the floor. MATT sits on the ground on top of their coats and layers.

MATT So, Gabe, explain—how come you need another kitchen down here?

GABRIEL Most Italian families have two kitchens in the house.

MATT For what, though?

GABRIEL I don't really know. I think it's like, they use the downstairs one if they're gonna be making a mess, or like, cooking fish.

MATT Fish.

GABRIEL Mm-hm. Yeah, so they don't go stinking up the whole upstairs.

MATT *(playing naïve)* Oh. So they need a whole other kitchen for that?

GABRIEL *(smiling)* Yeah, *just* for that …I don't know, it's like for when you have all of the relatives over for Christmas Eve, or like Confirmation parties. It's just more relaxed down here—so I guess people feel like they can let loose a bit more.

MATT Okay, I gotcha—kinda like a rec room type thing.

GABRIEL *(smiling)* Yeah, I guess. But we don't really do rec rooms, really…

MATT Oh-ho easy there, Alpha Romeo—excuse the *mangia*-cake.

GABRIEL Sh—I'm just saying it's different.

MATT I know. I'm just playing with you. Same idea, different name. "Or something."

GABRIEL Yeah, or something.

They laugh.

MATT *(playfully)* Shut up.

GABRIEL   You shut up.

   Pause.

MATT   I like how you get all pissed so easily.

GABRIEL   Um, for your information, it's you Irish people who get "pissed"—Italians get… passionate.

MATT   *(laughing)* Oh yeah? Oh yeah?—I'll give you Irish.

   He play-punches GABRIEL's shoulder. GABRIEL plays along. He then grabs both MATT's wrists, and slowly eases them down. The game dissolves— GABRIEL looks at him with a different intensity. GABRIEL is focused on getting details out of MATT, whereas MATT is becoming increasingly more "turned on." Each is aware of the other's growing focus. The mood shifts, as they connect more.

GABRIEL   Hey Matt…

MATT   What's up.

GABRIEL   Are you really gonna move away?

MATT   *(beat)* I think so. Probably. *(beat)* But let's not talk about that right now, okay?

GABRIEL   You have to?

MATT   "Have to" what?

GABRIEL   Move away.

MATT   Gabe, we move all the time—I told you this. You knew about this.

GABRIEL   I know, I know. *(beat)* Did he say when, though?—your dad?

MATT   Not really. He said it may not be 'til the end of next year… or it could be as soon as this spring. He won't know for a bit. *(beat)* Let's just stick to now, for now… Okay?

   GABRIEL lets go of his wrists.

GABRIEL   Yeah, you're right.

They look at each other, with an almost instant switch to a sexual tone. MATT leading, while GABRIEL coyly diverts.

MATT So… what do you wanna do now?

GABRIEL Umm, I guess we should start… building the universe.

MATT Gabe?

GABRIEL Where did you put that moon?

MATT Gabriel…

GABRIEL You had it, no?

MATT No it fell, remember? We… oh wait hold up, I think it must be on the floor behind you.

GABRIEL Matt, I think I would feel it, if it—

MATT reaches, cross-legged, across the floor pretending to search behind GABRIEL. GABRIEL leans back and turns away slightly. MATT remains perched over him.

MATT *(seductively)* You're a shit.

GABRIEL turns slightly to face him. Their faces are dangerously close.

GABRIEL *(playing along)* And you're a punk.

GABRIEL collapses MATT's arms, forcing him to fall on him. They send the planets rolling across the floor. MATT holds himself up on his arms, over GABRIEL. GABRIEL spreads his arms out. They both laugh. They switch to a more intimate and quiet tone.

GABRIEL What were you looking for again?

MATT The moon, dumbass.

GABRIEL Are you sure it wasn't Uranus?

MATT Ha, ha, you're so funny—Looking.

GABRIEL *(beat) (serious)* You're so, beautiful.

MATT   *(gently)* Shut up.

GABRIEL   For real, Matt.

MATT   So are you.

GABRIEL   No.

MATT   Yes.

>   *MATT gently leans in to kiss him.*

GABRIEL   Matt… I think I… I really like you.

MATT   That's cool—'cause, I like you too.

>   *After a moment they go back to building the project. They look at each other differently. The space between them is charged.*

Scene Nine

> *We resume with CONCETTA and MARCO from the previous scene. Only moments later. MARCO is still standing. CONCETTA enters as if nothing has happened, she has switched into a softer role. The "Good Mother." She stops when she sees MARCO.*

CONCETTA   Oh, Marco. *(beat)* Are you still here? I thought you would have left already. You can leave whenever you want, you know. I'm not making you stay. *(beat)* Are you going to be nice?

>   *MARCO is gob-smacked.*

MARCO   Am… I going to be… nice?

CONCETTA   Yes. Because if you can't be nice to your mother, you are going to have to go.

>   *MARCO takes this new state of hers, as an opportunity to hopefully connect without yelling. He carefully plays along.*

MARCO   Oh. Okay. Okay, Ma. I'll try to be nice. I'm sorry if I—

CONCETTA	*(a flash of anger)* A-a-a-a-a, DO NOT apologize to me. Please.
MARCO	Okay.

> CONCETTA *has an operatic look of pity on her face, as she swoops in to embrace him.*
>
> MARCO *has no idea how to respond, other than to allow himself to be mauled. After she lets go she sits him down. She moves around to sit at the table. She pulls out the rosary again and kisses a bead.*

CONCETTA	*(to the bead)* There. You see? Everything is better now.

> MARCO *looks as if he might be sick. He tries hard to maintain his composure.*

MARCO	That rosary… That's—?
CONCETTA	Gabriele's.
MARCO	Gabriel's rosary. *(beat)* How? I thought it was… How did you get it?
CONCETTA	*(dismissing)* What do you mean, how did I get it? I never lost it, Marco. Don't be strange.
MARCO	I'm—I just, I never thought I'd see it again. I'm surprised to see it.

> CONCETTA *ignores this last comment.*

CONCETTA	I keep it with me always, right here; *(indicates her chest)* I sewed a little black pocket inside my girdle to keep it in, right against my heart.

> MARCO *resists reacting.*

MARCO	Really. I didn't know that. *(beat)* That's really… um… nice.

> CONCETTA *glows.*

CONCETTA	Oh yes. Your brother's rosary is my salvation, you know. It is a promise. Just like the Virgin Mary said when she appeared with it for the first time on the mountain; "Only if you pray with this

every day will you be saved. Pray the rosary and keep it sacred, and even your most difficult prayer will be answered." It is a *promise*, Marco. Your brother understands that. That's why he always keeps it with him.

MARCO looks as if he might start crying.

MARCO Yes—he *did*.

CONCETTA Because it protects him. It connects him to the Mother Mary—mother of us all. *(beat)* You remember how it was this rosary, that made the miracle for him?

MARCO Yes. I remember.

CONCETTA takes flight. Inflated, in her re-telling, she moves around the room, as if this might be an aria. MARCO carefully tries to de-rail her from the story, throughout, but she speaks over him.

CONCETTA Remember we had gone to Brooklyn, for your cousin Sandra's wedding all those years ago. He was still little—you both were, remember?

MARCO —Ma, please. I want to talk about something here.

CONCETTA You and him had gone to the store with your cousin Ralphy, to get cigarettes for the men. Me and your Aunt Gina—God rest her soul—were making oven vegetables in her basement kitchen.

MARCO You don't have to tell this again, I know the story.

CONCETTA We were cutting and peeling, and all of a sudden Raphaele come running in, and the next thing I know, I was—No. NO. That's not right. See, it's wrong the way I'm telling it... see? YOU—it starts to fade in my head if I don't get to tell it.

MARCO —Why are you doing this now?

CONCETTA SHHHHHH!!

She quickly gathers herself and re-enters her state.

	No, no… it's all right, it's back. I do remember: Gina heard it first, before the basement door opened. From inside she heard the truck tires squeal, and then the people on the street screaming: Oh my God—it's a child. It's a kid under there! And before we could move, Ralphy was in like a ghost—crying so he couldn't breathe. Gina grabbed him and shook him: "What happened Raphaele? What's wrong?!". He opened his mouth and said: "Gabriele's dead." My bladder spilled on my chair. Gabriele's dead—and all at once my feet were on the front porch, my apron wet and steaming, and an onion still in my hand: I stood there. I could not move. People around the truck. People yelling. My sister screaming at me from the street: "You stay where you are! Don't come here!" And I stood there, realized your baby brother had just been rolled over by a pick-up truck—and I had a smile on my face—
MARCO	–Ma, please…
CONCETTA	—A SMILE on my face. The smile was because of God; He was present at that moment. My faith was on my face. I smiled, because I knew I couldn't move even if I wanted to. Two angels with soot on their faces held my feet down like cement. And then the miracle; the crowd opened, and from under the truck your brother came out like a painting, unharmed. He smiled at me—the same smile, because he knew God wouldn't have let him die. He ran to me and hugged my legs, while all those people beat their heads not believing what they had seen. He told me God had saved him, and I asked him how? And he reached into his pocket and pulled out this rosary. "*That's* how," he said. Remember how when he was little he always used to keep it in his pocket? (*beat*) He was such a good boy. Your brother was blessed, you know. He wasn't like the other boys; he was… protected.

MARCO *(beat)* Why is that the only story you tell when you talk about him?

CONCETTA *(oblivious)* And then me and Gabriele walked to the front of the truck—the man who was driving was crying like a baby with his head on the steering wheel. And I picked up Gabriele, so the man could see, "Stop your crying, my boy is not dead. God is bigger than your truck." And that man stared; like this. He started to cry even harder. I took Gabriele's hand and put it on his arm, "Go home mister, we are all right."

MARCO And then did you light incense at his feet, Ma? *(beat)*

    He gets up.

My God, you're turning it into a movie. It wasn't like that at all: I was there in case you forgot. I saw it all.

CONCETTA *(acknowledging him, distantly)* Oh I know. Do not think I have forgotten you were there. I know about you.

MARCO He *slipped* Ma—that's all! He ran ahead and tripped on the curb. The guy driving the truck slammed on the brakes because he saw Gabe go down just as he was passing. He was confused. Ralphy ran—everyone went crazy. They thought Gabe was under the truck—but nobody actually looked first. He wasn't even close to the wheels—he was near the sewer grate thing. He froze when he heard everyone freaking out. He stood up when he heard you.

    CONCETTA finally faces him. Accusingly.

CONCETTA On the way back to the house, I saw you. Standing on the curb, all dark, with your hands in your pockets like you did something wrong. *(beat)* Just looking at us like a stranger. You had not run to him, to me—you just watched through the whole thing.

MARCO	I was a kid, goddammit! I was in shock or something! I didn't know what to do! Okay?! Oh, but I guess in your story that's how you need to see things, huh? If he was the saint, well, then of course I had to be the little demon, right? Is that right, Ma?!

CONCETTA looks straight ahead. She says nothing.

Sure, that's right—unplug on me again: it's not what you want to hear, so ignore it all. But I'm telling you one thing, Ma—what you remember, are not the FACTS. What you think is crazy—this is crazy! Why do you always stop at him as a little boy? Huh? What about the rest of his life?… Like what he grew up to be?

CONCETTA	You need to learn to shut up your stupid MOUTH!!
MARCO	Why is this house empty, Ma? Why is he gone?… Speak!—
CONCETTA	Shut you BE QUIET!!!
MARCO	No, no more.
CONCETTA	You go now—your plane is leaving.
MARCO	Forget about that—the plane is gone. I'm not going anywhere. *(beat)* Did you forget the rest of the story? *(beat)* Did you make yourself forget?! Is that even possible?
CONCETTA	You FORGET how to speak to your MOTHER!
MARCO	Well jesuschrist—Where is she?! Look at me.

He wheels her around to face him.

LOOK at me! *(beat)* I don't know who I'm speaking to anymore. Show me my mother, and I'll speak to her like I used to, okay?

CONCETTA	*(pleading)* You want to kill me, Marco? Why— What are you doing to me?

She attempts to caress his face

MARCO (*revolted by her touch*) No, okay?! NO. You can't forget—I will not ALLOW you to rewrite, understand? *I* don't have that choice—Gabriel doesn't have that choice. There is one truth, Ma. One. Our stories are not the same, because you are ignoring the biggest part. You leave out what we did. What WE did to him. You and Pa and me. It's because of us that he went and—

CONCETTA (*pushing away from him*) NNNOOOO!!! Don't open your mouth!

MARCO —Ma!

CONCETTA You don't know what you are saying!

MARCO YOU'RE the one who doesn't know, I KNOW what I am talking about!

CONCETTA WHAT?! *What*, Marco. *Per l'amore di Dio,* what are you talking about?

Lights snap to black.

Scene Ten

Isolate PAOLO standing on the bridge—motionless, he looks out past everything.

Lights fade on him very slowly.

Scene Eleven

Three years earlier. The upstairs kitchen. The set table is used to indicate the sink and counter. An earlier time; when the family home was overflowing with life, and humour. CONCETTA dries dishes, her back to the audience. She wears a floral patterned duster over her mourning—in order to help distinguish a different time. She hums quietly. GABRIEL enters wearing jeans and no shirt. He dries his hair with a small towel. He has a T-shirt tucked in the back of his jeans. The tone is playful.

CONCETTA Gabriele! *Aie*—come on, watch you don't put hair on the plates!

GABRIEL I won't, relax.

CONCETTA Relax—move.

He shuffles over.

GABRIEL How do I look?

CONCETTA Like a wet dog.

GABRIEL Oh-ho—*mille grazie*.

CONCETTA Handsome. You know already, I don't need to tell you. *(beat)* So, where are you going again?

GABRIEL I told you already / like five thousand times.

CONCETTA / I know you told me already, and now look how you are gonna tell me again. I'm old, remember? My brain no work no more.

GABRIEL Ugh. I'm going out with Sara.

CONCETTA *Sara*, huh? Pretty Sara. Where?

GABRIEL What?

CONCETTA Where? Where are you going?—I'm speaking English, even.

GABRIEL Holy inquisition—we're going to a club or something.

CONCETTA A club?

GABRIEL Ohmygod—yes.

CONCETTA Don't "ohmagod" me. I am just asking—I'm not eating you or nothing.

GABRIEL *(play-flirting)* Why, do you want to come with us? You want to come out dancing?

CONCETTA *(smiling)* …Gabriele, mah please. Stop talking and go get ready if you're gonna get ready.

GABRIEL *(He comes up behind her and tickles her.)* Huh? What'd you say? Maybe some hot guy will whisper how beautiful you are... *(He zerberts her arm—to drive her crazy.)*

CONCETTA Gabriele!

> *She chases him swatting him with the dish towel. They both love it.*

Now you're gonna get it, you crazy.

> *She spanks his butt playfully. He spins around and tries to lift her in a bear hug.*

Oh my—Gabriele! Put me down! You gonna break your back.

GABRIEL Uggrh! Whew, only Marco could do this without breaking his—

CONCETTA Shut up you! Nobody told to you to lift your mother—are you crazy?

> *They both laugh. She is embarrassed.*

GABRIEL You're not that heavy, Ma—I was faking.

CONCETTA Ah, ah—no swearing in the house.

> *GABRIEL has no idea what she has misunderstood. He starts laughing:*

GABRIEL What?

> *MARCO and PAOLO enter in grubby work clothes with greasy hands.*

PAOLO What's with all the screaming in here?

> *He and MARCO enter with cold cuts and bread and start building a sandwich.*

CONCETTA *(indicating a crazy head)* Your son is a *pazzo*. I was gonna bring out the food.

PAOLO Don't worry. We can do it, right Marco?

> *MARCO already has coldcuts in his mouth.*

MARCO   We could hear you from outside—sounded like you were killing a pig in here.

GABRIEL   No: just trying to lift Ma.

> *CONCETTA slaps him with the dish towel. MARCO laughs. PAOLO suppresses his laughter, but CONCETTA clocks it.*

CONCETTA   *(to PAOLO)* …Oh really, you too, even? Who next, huh? Mah-please—

PAOLO   *(suppressing his smile, to GABRIEL)* That's right, you watch your mouth there, Jerry Lewis—before I give you one. *(to MARCO)* And you, be quiet and stop smiling.

MARCO   Pa, come on, you know that was funny shit.

PAOLO   *Aie! (He swats MARCO, then he looks at her, playfully helpless.)* Concettina, what am I supposed to do? All of a sudden everyone talks like we're on a loading dock or something—you better watch your mouths!

CONCETTA   Psh! And who did they learn it from?—Anyway, it's because of you all that I'm fatter, you know. If I was by myself I would be full with just two olives and half a bread: cooking for you all is making me a pig.

PAOLO   Never mind what they say—it's good on you. This way, if you slip on the ice, it will cushion your bones.

> *He kisses her head.*

MARCO   Yeah and crack the sidewalk!

> *He jokingly runs to hide behind GABRIEL, CONCETTA and PAOLO take turns slapping MARCO on the back of the head. It is all handled playfully.*

CONCETTA   Ah yes? You think you are too old to get a slap from me? Even when you leave this house, you'll still be my babies!

GABRIEL gets a big swat in the ass from CONCETTA.

GABRIEL Ma, and her endless supply of wooden spoons flying through the air at us forever…

More laughter.

MARCO *(laughing)* Total—*(He does a ninja spoon-throwing move.)*

PAOLO You two are so funny comedians: that I almost forgot to pay.

A collective BEAT. No one understands this comment.

GABRIEL What?

CONCETTA What?

They all burst out laughing.

PAOLO Hahaha, you know what I mean. *(to MARCO)* Anyhow, I don't know why you're laughing—what are you, five years old?

MARCO What, it was funny. Ho-ly.

PAOLO Don't be smart, Marco—you still got work to do. Enough playing around: those bolts are not going to tighten themselves. Stop with the chip-chap and let's go, you.

PAOLO smacks him on the back of the head as he leaves. Once MARCO has seen that he is clear of view, he gives him the Italian hand-to-elbow 'Fuck-you.' CONCETTA sees this.

CONCETTA Marco!

MARCO Well…? What's he gotta be like that for?

CONCETTA You don't do that, okay? Now go help him and be nice.

MARCO doesn't even want the rest of his sandwich. He slugs back the water, and follows his father out. He play punches GABRIEL on the way out. After a beat CONCETTA looks at GABRIEL. He sticks out his bottom lip, trying to butter-up his mother.

CONCETTA And you. Don't even bother with that lip.

GABRIEL Ma, we're just playing around. You're gorgeous—and you know it.

CONCETTA Puh, okay please. All I got to say is that I was ninety pounds when I married your father. A wind could have blown me over.

GABRIEL Yeah, and look at you now; Stunning—like Sophia Loren.

CONCETTA Oh yes, Mr. Smartmouth, well either dry the dishes you got wet or go wherever you got to go.

GABRIEL *(kisses her)* Okay, if Sara gets here before I come down, let her in.

CONCETTA *(sarcastic)* No, really? I'm a cave-woman: I was going to leave her out in the cold. Mah-please, go do what you gotta do and stop wasting time.

GABRIEL goes to exit.

As if I am gonna leave your girlfriend out in the night.

GABRIEL *(before he gets to the door)* She's not my girlfriend.

CONCETTA What? Come here for a second, Gabriele. Now, what do you mean?

GABRIEL *(coming back in)* What Ma? Just tell me—I gotta get ready.

GABRIEL pulls the tight T-shirt over his head.

CONCETTA So?

GABRIEL ..."So?" *(beat)* So what?

CONCETTA Sit down with me for one minute.

GABRIEL Ma, come on...

CONCETTA   A-a-a. Sit when I tell you to sit. *(He does.)* That's right. *(calmly)* Look. You are not a baby no more. You don't got to pretend no more with me.

> Beat. GABRIEL shifts gears, unsure whether his mother is hinting at something else.

GABRIEL   Pretend what...?

CONCETTA   You are allowed to have girlfriends you know. It is normal at your age.

GABRIEL   *(carefully)* I know. But she's not.

CONCETTA   Sara? Come on—you go out with her all the time. She's very pretty, always calling for you on the phone and everything.

GABRIEL   Yeah... so?

CONCETTA   Gabriele, please, I was not born the other day—I'm not stupid you know. A mother knows all these things.

GABRIEL   *(His heart sinks a bit.)* I know.

CONCETTA   You can tell me.

GABRIEL   *(carefully)* I would, Ma. I would tell you if she was, but she's not, though. My girlfriend. She's not, okay?

> They study each others' eyes. CONCETTA is picking up a vibe that she cannot ignore.

CONCETTA   She's not, huh?

GABRIEL   No. She's not.

> Pause.

CONCETTA   Then, what is she?

GABRIEL   *(innocently)* I don't know, um, a girl?

CONCETTA   Gabriele... you know what I mean.

GABRIEL   Fine. She's my best friend.

> Silence.

CONCETTA   Your best friend?

GABRIEL   Yes.

CONCETTA   How can she be your best friend?

GABRIEL   What do you mean, *how*? She's a really good friend, and… but not like that. Ma, we get along 'cause she understands me.

> *CONCETTA tries to understand.*

CONCETTA   …What is to understand?

GABRIEL   *(trying to refrain from crying, quietly)* Why are you pushing this, Ma? *(beat)* Why?

> *CONCETTA says nothing, but looks away.*

She's gonna be here soon. Can I go finish getting ready?

CONCETTA   *(distracted)* Yes.

> *For a moment they stand, looking into each others eyes. GABRIEL turns and leaves. CONCETTA slowly goes back to drying dishes. The doorbell rings, and lights shift as CONCETTA resumes her earlier position where she left off with MARCO.*

Scene Twelve

> *Present. Upstairs kitchen. MARCO and CONCETTA continue from where they left off in their first scene. They are breathing hard, like two wrestlers in a ring. CONCETTA has shifted yet again, into a more grounded, laser-like opponent.*

CONCETTA   What. Tell me. Tell me what you are talking about.

> *MARCO noticing a shift in her.*

MARCO   *(carefully)* Ma, look. I'm not doing this to hurt you. I'm not, I swear. But you need to understand why—

CONCETTA   *Marco. (beat)* Say what you have to. Tell me.

MARCO Ma, I think you gotta talk to someone about all of this—A person who knows about these things: so they can help you.

CONCETTA So they can help me? *(beat)* You are so smart. Who do I got to talk to? Who? Who knows better than me about these things? Who?—*You*? *(beat)* Be quiet, and don't speak of things you don't understand.

MARCO He's *gone*, Ma / —But you don't accept that—

CONCETTA I will not tell you again.

MARCO —Okay Ma, you tell me where is he then?! Where is Gabriel?—

CONCETTA turns on him. Vitriolic.

CONCETTA ENOUGH!! No more! I will not speak of him to you. I will not hear you about this. *(beat)* You. You will never understand what he did to me. Never. If I was going to start to even try to tell you—to tell you, I am sure my own living heart would squeeze, would pour out through my eyes, my ears, my fingernails! My, my… *How* can I?… *(beat)*

She climbs up onto the kitchen table while speaking:

I. Am. Hot. With him. You cannot understand. That beautiful boy did came from me. He boils under my… everything.

CONCETTA desperately looks around herself, to try and illustrate her pain. She abruptly stops. She focuses on a space between her and reality;

EVERYTHING is him. So you can not speak …to me… about him. *(beat)* I cannot hear you.

Lights shift. Music. MARCO disappears.

Scene Thirteen

CONCETTA alone on top of the table. She grabs her stomach in pain, a flash, she exhales. She looks out with intensity. She reaches into her apron pockets and comes out with two handfuls of flour. She throws them on the table before her. She takes in a deep breath and exhales. A huge mound of dough (the size of a small child) falls from above landing before her.

Lights slowly rise on the ground floor below and in front of her, revealing a parka and a winter coat surrounded by project materials, several painted Styrofoam moons and planets, many of them are still unfinished. In the shadows of the dimly-lit basement, leaning against one of the unfinished walls, the two young men are revealed. Their costumes should signal that it is a week after their last scene. GABRIEL is pushed up against MATT who stands with his back against the wall. GABRIEL is kissing his neck.

MATT *(referring to his sexual excitement)* Gabe—honestly man, you're killing me.

GABRIEL Is that a good thing?

CONCETTA kneels and begins kneading the dough.

GABRIEL puts his hands into the back of MATT's jeans. The kissing becomes passionate and desperate. They make out fiercely—almost as if it were keeping reality at bay.

CONCETTA begins praying* quietly under the boys' scene. Her prayer and the boy's dialogue should be delivered simultaneously. She is in the religious ecstasy that comes with direct prayer.

MATT Mmmmhh. *(out of breath)* Gabe?

GABRIEL *(still kissing his neck)* Mm-hmmm?

MATT Gabe... do you feel me?

GABRIEL   Yeah.

MATT   I'm hard.

GABRIEL   Me too.

MATT   I mean really hard.

GABRIEL   Stop talking.

They continue making out, with increasing passion.

MATT   Mmm… Gabe?

GABRIEL   *(while his mouth kisses MATT's exposed stomach and hips)* Mmm-hm…

MATT   Where's your family again?

GABRIEL   I told you, my father's at the factory, and my ma's at my cousin's who had the baby.

MATT   What about your bro?

GABRIEL   My brother's at work—Why?

MATT   Good. So we're okay here?

GABRIEL   Yeah, why?

MATT   Well… we're both hard.

GABRIEL   Yeah.

CONCETTA finishes her prayer. Lights snap to black on her.

MATT pulls GABRIEL up to look him in the face.

MATT   *(beat)* I want more this time.

GABRIEL   More? What do you mean? *(beat)* Like… *more*? Are you serious?

MATT   I want you closer. *(He kisses him deeply.)* I want to go with you.

He kisses his eyes, his nose, then sensually licks GABRIEL's lips.

GABRIEL   *(completely taken)* Uhhh …Holy shit.

(l to r:) Marc Bendavid, Toni Ellwand and Kristopher Turner, from the Buddies in Bad Times production, March, 2006. *photo by Dennis Horn*

MATT   No clothes, or anything. *(beat)* No space between us.

> MATT puts his hands into the front of GABRIEL'S pants.

GABRIEL   Aw God... Matt... we can't.

MATT   Gabe. *(He pulls him closer.)* ...We already are.

> They make out with building intensity.

Do you want to?

GABRIEL   Shhhh.

MATT   I'm serious.

GABRIEL   For real?

MATT   Gabriel, yes.

GABRIEL   Now? Just like... this?

> MATT removes his own shirt.

MATT   *(smiling)* Like this.

> GABRIEL looks at him for a beat, then takes off his shirt. They both face each other up on their knees. MATT kisses GABRIEL's chest and shoulders. GABRIEL raises his arms above his head. MATT unbuttons GABRIEL's jeans, and begins to pulls them down. They stand up together to get the jeans off. They stand close, facing each other. MATT takes off his own jeans. For a second they stand in their underwear. They kiss, as the lights begin to dim. With his back to the audience, GABRIEL removes his own underwear, MATT smiles and drops his boxers. They both make their way back to the floor, as the lights slowly dim:
>
> CONCETTA makes her way off stage holding the dough as if it were a baby.

CONCETTA   *(text spoken under the dialogue above) Padre nostro che sei nei cieli; ti prego con tutto ciò di cui sono fatta, che tutto in questa famiglia sia come mi hai promesso.

Ho sacrificato troppo, e non perché fossi lasciata con niente. Troppi sacrifici—molti di più di quanto puoi immaginare. E dopo tutta questa devozione, ci sono certe cose che vedo—che non posso accettare. Davvero. E per questo Ti chiedo—Ti prego—Ti prego di darmi la forza—non per accettare. No. Anzi, invece Ti prego di darmi la forza di non vedere. Voglio essere cieca, sì, è questo che voglio da Te. Tutti pregano per la vista, ma io ho bisogno che me la togli in modo da non vedere niente di quelle cose. Aiutaci a trovare ancora una volta, la chiarezza nella nostra vita. Aiutaci a trovare, ancora una volta la strada giusta da prendere. (beat) E Tu; Maria santissima—perché anche tu sei una mamma—ti prego forte per mio figlio Gabriel: fa che tutto ciò che vedo in lui, non sia quello che ho intuito essere. Fa che tutte le mie speranze per Gabriel, non risultino perdute... Troppi sacrifici. Ascoltami, Ti supplico. Amen.

(TRANSLATION: Our Father who lives in heaven; I pray to you with all that I am made of, that everything in this family turns out like you have promised me. I have sacrificed too much, and not so I should be left with nothing. Too many sacrifices—more than even you could know. And after all this devotion, there are certain things that I see, that I can not accept. Truly. And for this I pray to you—I pray for the strength—not to accept, no. Instead I pray for the strength not to see. Blindness, this is what I need from you. Everyone else prays for sight, but I need mine taken away from me so I don't see things. Help us find once again, your clarity in our lives. Help us find, once again, the right road to take. *(beat)* And to you; Holy Mary—because you too are a mother—I pray hard for my son Gabriel: that all that I see in him, is not as I understand it to be. I pray that all my hopes for Gabriel don't find themselves lost... Too many sacrifices. Listen to me, please. I beg you. Amen.)

ACT II

Scene Fourteen

The unfinished basement kitchen. Lights slowly rise to reveal MATT and GABRIEL on the concrete floor a week after Scene Thirteen. They are naked, lying beside each other on a blanket. Their clothes (different from what they wore in Scene Thirteen) sit in two piles on the floor beside them. On the other side of them, rests the nearly-completed model of the universe. A contraption with painted styrofoam planets attached to coat-hanger wires that extend out from a base. A few planets are still not in place. Research papers are spread out beside a school binder. They have just finished having sex — only their second time together. They hold their hands together raised in the air above them. They look at their joined hands. Silence.

GABRIEL …Beautiful…

MATT *(gently)* Shhh …

GABRIEL You.

MATT You.

Silence.

So…?

GABRIEL Yeah?

MATT What do we do now?

GABRIEL Mm, we have to finish putting the universe together.

They share a little laugh. MATT sits up.

MATT Seriously, Gabriel, what do we do with this?… With us?

GABRIEL What do you mean?

MATT I mean… obviously we *like* each other.

GABRIEL Yeah, we do.

MATT	Are we supposed to hide that? Like, I mean is that something we can actually hide?
GABRIEL	I don't know—why are you asking this?
MATT	I don't know. I'm not really sure what's happening, right—but I like it. Gabriel I really like being with you, and it bugs me that we have to hide it—that's all.
GABRIEL	I know, but—just think of it like… I don't know—we're not hiding it; we're just keeping it for ourselves. Safe.
MATT	Call it what you want, it still sucks. Gabe, we're eighteen—we're not kids anymore, you know?
GABRIEL	What does that have to do with anything?
MATT	Everything. It means we can't pretend not to be who we are anymore. We have to, I don't know—accept it.
GABRIEL	Matt, it's not that simple.
MATT	Well, it has to be. Christ, if our families can't accept us, then—screw them, we can move out. We're allowed to now. Legally, we're adults.
GABRIEL	Yeah, I know. But. I love my family… I need them in my life, you know? I don't want to live without them—I can't imagine that. *(beat)* They love me, Matt.
MATT	Look, I know, same here. They love us; but only as long as we're what they want us to be.
GABRIEL	Matt…
MATT	Well…?
	GABRIEL is silent. He looks very heavy with consideration.
	What's wrong?
GABRIEL	Nothing.
MATT	Why aren't you talking?

GABRIEL	'Cause I don't know what to say.
MATT	Say anything. *(beat)* Do you like being with me?
GABRIEL	Matt, you know I do.
MATT	Is it us having sex?
GABRIEL	No. *(beat)* I've never felt anything like that before.
MATT	Me neither. It feels really… *(beat)* Gabe, what are we?
GABRIEL	What.
MATT	Are we gay?

GABRIEL reacts as if he's heard the worst word.

GABRIEL	Shh, no—don't! Matt, don't say that.
MATT	What, I'm just asking, does this automatically make us— / gay?
GABRIEL	/ Please! Don't say that in here—Matt, I'm not playing.
MATT	Why are you freaking? Nobody's here, it's just—
GABRIEL	Knock on wood.
MATT	What? Why?
GABRIEL	Just do it. Please.

MATT looks at him for a beat.

MATT	*(mischievously)* 'Kay, no prob. I'll knock on some wood for you.

MATT reaches across to touch GABRIEL's penis, but he pushes him off quickly.

GABRIEL	Don't, okay?! I'm serious, Matt. Don't say that stuff in here. You can't do that—just knock on wood, 'cause you said it. For real, please.

GABRIEL gets up and puts on his underwear.

MATT	*(He knocks on wood.)* There. Okay? *(beat)* What's with the wood? Holy, you're so serious.

GABRIEL I'm sorry—you don't understand: Once you say it out loud we can never escape it.

MATT "Escape it?" What are you talking about? Gabe, honestly you're starting to weird me out.

He gets up and puts on his underwear. As if getting ready to leave.

GABRIEL Matt. Matt, I'm sorry—okay, look: My whole life, whenever we said something bad in the house, anything that could sound like a curse: like "Cancer" or "I wish I was dead"—understand? If we said anything like that out loud, my mother would freak and tell us to knock on wood.

MATT Wow. That's some crazy shit.

GABRIEL No, it's just Sicilian. *(beat)* Anyhow, she was totally serious: "Knock on wood"—and she wouldn't let up until we did it.

MATT Where did she get this?

GABRIEL Back in Sicily, the old people used to say that you had to knock on wood to make the trees deaf to what had just been said: to stop the curse.

MATT Trees?

GABRIEL They said that the trees would turn into lumber at some point, and that wood is what you would end up building your house with. And your bed, and your kitchen table—get it?

MATT No.

GABRIEL Everything you say becomes ingrained in the wood you build your home with—so that, if you didn't knock on wood, you would be destined to live in a house with no peace, and lie in a bed of discomfort. End-quote.

MATT Okay… I think I see now. Well, I'm sorry.

GABRIEL It's cool—you didn't know. *(beat)* I'm sorry I snapped; It's just, like, I know it sounds weird—

	and I know it's Old-World superstition, but when you hear these things all your life, they stick with you.
MATT	Hm. Kinda like the curses stick in the wood.
GABRIEL	*(beat)* That's it—exactly… I never thought of that.
MATT	*(beat)* Okay, so I guess telling your family is out of the question.
GABRIEL	Matt.
MATT	I'm kidding.
GABRIEL	*(beat)* Seriously though, I don't think I could ever tell them. I have nightmares about it.
MATT	Shyeah. My parents would totally flip out if I said anything, could you imagine? My dad's a cop for chrissake.
GABRIEL	It would be bad is all I know.
MATT	All's I know is, I don't want to screw this up with you. This is good—whatever it is. We don't have to say anything to anyone.
GABRIEL	For real?
MATT	Yeah sure. People pretend all the time, look around you—everyone pretends. But then there's the people who fake—and faking is worse than lying… my mom *fakes* that she still loves my dad, but I can tell that she hates her life with him. She's just too weak to do anything about it now; so she'll stick it out until she dies, probably.
GABRIEL	She would rather die unhappy than do something?
MATT	It looks that way, I guess.

GABRIEL is struck by the sadness of that idea.

Anyhow, it's all good. You and me, we can just wait till we're alone together to be real with each other—screw everyone else, right?

GABRIEL	*(distracted)* Yeah, I guess.
MATT	We'll just make times when we can be alone, here, in our little kitchen.
GABRIEL	*(laughing)* "Our little kitchen?" This basement?
MATT	Sure, why not? We just have to use our imagination a bit to make it all work, you know?
GABRIEL	You lost me.
MATT	Like, it's actually kinda good that there's nothing here, you know? No walls or stuff.
GABRIEL	What, you don't like walls?
MATT	No, it's just that it's… empty. It makes it easier for us to lie here and imagine what it could be like.

MATT starts to get into his own idea.

	Check it out: Close your eyes for a sec. *(beat)* Gabe, come on, do it. Good. Now imagine like this is our own house—you and me. This is our kitchen—actually no, this would be your kitchen—I would have the rec room, right?
GABRIEL	*(smiling)* Shut—you're such an ass.
MATT	Go with me on this. *(beat)* Please. Keep your eyes closed. Wait till you get used to the blackness, and then you'll start to see everything come into focus—imagine. The door, the table, the chairs, the fridge.
GABRIEL	The sink…
MATT	The dishes you chose are drying on the counter.
GABRIEL	Okay…
MATT	Picture all of it so clearly that it feels real—every little thing… the calendar on the wall, the clock.
GABRIEL	Okay, I'm there.
MATT	*(gently)* Nope, you're *here*. Open your eyes. Slowly.

GABRIEL does.

Well?... Can you still see it?

Throughout the following, GABRIEL slowly becomes transported by the game, fuelled by MATT's intensity and focus.

GABRIEL I think I do, yeah.

MATT Come on, you do. *(beat)* Do you know where you are?

GABRIEL Yeah... we're in the...

MATT You're in Gabriel's kitchen.

GABRIEL I am... Gabriel's kitchen... it's so real. *(beat)* This is crazy—

He is too afraid to go further, and opens his eyes. He turns away slightly. MATT gently pulls him back in.

MATT *(serious)* Gabe, come on, you have to trust me, okay? *(beat)* You're safe with me.

MATT gently brings him down to sit on the ground again. He sits behind him with his legs around him. They both face out.

You have to let yourself go a bit, and then if you let yourself imagine hard, like—it'll almost be real; you'll feel like you can almost step out into it. Just close your eyes.

GABRIEL does.

Lean back. Feel me breathing against you... okay.

GABRIEL *(after a moment, he smiles)* Oh my God, Matthew... holy...

MATT Do you see?

GABRIEL I can see it... yeah. *(beat)* I'm here.

MATT Where...?

GABRIEL In my kitchen.

MATT Cool. Where am I? Do you see me?

GABRIEL I feel you.

MATT Yeah, but I bet from now on, we'll be able feel each other even if we're not in the same room. See? As long as we have our basement we can imagine whatever we want—screw the real world, 'cause it sucks anyway.

GABRIEL *(back to the game)* So wait, are you saying you're not here with me?

MATT Well, I am; but I'm not.

GABRIEL Why are you so complicated?

MATT Shut up, you love it.

> *MATT gives him a quick peck.*

GABRIEL *(beat)* Are you here in my kitchen?

MATT Nope.

GABRIEL Are you in Matt's rec room?

MATT Nope… I went out back, onto our field and I'm lying in the grass.

GABRIEL We have a field?

MATT Yeah man, look over there.

> *He indicates in the direction of the audience.*

Look, we have a huge window right there, so we can look out onto the field. Tall grass—so green, it's almost blue. *(beat)* Can you see me? I'm waving to you. There I am.

GABRIEL I see you, Matt. *(beat)* I can see you.

MATT *(beat)* Well then, come to me, Gabriel.

> *They turn to each other and look into each other faces for a beat.*

And… here… I… am.

> *He kisses GABRIEL. They start laughing. They wrap their legs around each other and put their arms over the other's shoulders so that they are face to face.*

GABRIEL	You know what?
MATT	What?
GABRIEL	You're crazy.
MATT	Oh yeah, you know what?
GABRIEL	What?
MATT	*(beat)* You are beautiful. *(beat)* For real.

They stare at each other and begin to trace each other's faces in a relaxed way. After a moment, GABRIEL puts his head on MATT's chest, and MATT embraces him.

Cross into:

Scene Fifteen

Present. Upstairs kitchen. CONCETTA and MARCO continue from where they left off.

MARCO	I can't talk about him, because I don't understand? Huh, Ma? That's what you're telling me?
CONCETTA	My head is hurting.
MARCO	I don't *understand*? What, do you think this has been easy for me?
CONCETTA	Listen: You could never understand the suffering of a mother.
MARCO	Of course! It all comes back to "suffering," doesn't it? Suffer like a saint.
CONCETTA	I don't want to talk to you.
MARCO	Jesus Christ! We've all suffered, Ma. You are not the only one. Pa is also suffering—did you ever stop to think of that? For chrissake, look at me! What about me? *(beat)* I don't even know what to do any more! I'm afraid to come back here—I'm afraid to leave here. Ma, do you even know what I go back home to? Nothing! I have nothing! No friends, no family—I've screwed everything up,

	because of what happened here. That's what you don't understand.
CONCETTA	What are you talking about.
MARCO	For the past three years, my life away from here has been shit. Okay? A joke. *(beat)* God, you probably thought that after the holidays, whenever I go back, that I am happy away from this place—but I'm not. I just bring all the sadness with me. *(beat)* I thought moving away from this house would fix everything. I tried to start over. I wanted things to get right so bad. I tried to plan everything I could, so that I could make sure everything would fit together perfectly. School, then the job, then the girlfriend who would become the wife: who would make me babies: that would give you…
CONCETTA	Marco…
MARCO	I was like a worker. I went crazy trying to find exactly the right people to fill in all the empty parts—to pull all the pieces together. I went through people like water; if they weren't exactly what I needed them to be; I turned away. These were people who were good to me—but it actually made me sick to see how easily people could care for me. *(beat)* One day, you know, I just took stock: Everyone and everything I'd cut off… and, you know what? It tired me out. I ached—my whole body; like a murderer. *(beat)* I have made it so that no one wants to be around me anymore. Just like you and Pa. CONCETTA *stares at him.* *(noticing her stare)* Ma…?
CONCETTA	*(beat)* What am I supposed to do? What do you want from me?
MARCO	I want you to deal with shit. Reality! I feel like I have the weight of everything on me. I can't do it alone any more. *I* found him, Ma—I'm the only

one who carries that, okay? It has screwed up my life, so that I have nothing that makes me happy. I'm not like you—I am not strong enough to pretend as if / it didn't—

CONCETTA / StopstopstopSTOP! Enough! Listen to you! *(beat)* What are you? You carried everything for three years? *Reality*? At least you had SOMETHING! But me? *(beat)* I had nothing *real* to carry. I don't remember as much as you, Marco. All right? I missed the day of the funeral— because of the needle they gave me! Did you forget that?! I MISSED it! When I could see straight again, everything had been finished already—without me. You must understand that!

MARCO —Ma—

CONCETTA THAT is all the *reality* I was allowed! And I do my best Marco, I do my best with the nothing that I have—ALL RIGHT? One day I come home from the shopping and you won't let me past you; you say something to me and my eyes go dark. That is all. The next time I come home—from the hospital this time—there are four days I don't remember living. My house smells like Lysol, and... and someone is trying to tell to me that my boy, MY baby boy—my son—is gone—forever. That HE did put himself in the cold ground forever ...someone even put all his pictures in a box, and hid them where I don't know. This is what I have, Marco. So what reality then? Huh? *(beat)* How dare you? How DARE you?! No, no—you tell me what reality I am supposed to be in. Please, for true, make me understand *where* is this reality—and I will go live in it. But until someone tells me how to do better—THIS is my reality! This house is my... this broadloom, this doorways, this ceilings, this windows—

MARCO And the basement kitchen.

CONCETTA —PLEASE STOP!

MARCO   Look Ma, I'm sorry—I am sorry but / you need to face—

CONCETTA   / I don't want to hear that! Do not be sorry! I don't need for anyone to be sorry—I… Need… My boy back!—That's all I need. I need back my Gabriel, please! I need to put my knees on his grave and I need to pull him up from out of the ground and I need to hit him!—

MARCO covers his ears without realizing it.

I *hate* him, Marco. I do. I hate him. God forgive me—but it's true. Look at what he did! Look at us! Look! He didn't give us no chance to turn for him. He decided everything. He never gave me no chance—he finished everything for everyone.

MARCO   Ma.

CONCETTA   He destroyed our lives on that day. Look at us now, Marco. What are we? What is left of us? Nothing! *(beat)* He had no right, Marco. *(beat)* I *gave* him his life…

Pause.

MARCO   You're not wrong.

CONCETTA   But I am not right?

MARCO is silent.

A-ha… you don't know what to say? Me too, Marco—now our conversation can start.

Silence. Then:

I am listening.

MARCO   *(confused)* …What? I don't—

CONCETTA   Give me your reality. Tell me what you saw that day… when you found him.

MARCO is suddenly terrified by her audience. He is paralyzed at the thought of having to reveal all the details.

MARCO   I can't do this, Ma— / I'm sorry I can't, I can't—

CONCETTA   / Yes. You never told me. I pleaded with you to tell me, and you never. Marco. *(beat)* I need to know, so I don't imagine anymore. Tell me what you saw in the basement. Everything; clear like pictures. Tell me.

MARCO   *(afraid)* Please… Ma…

CONCETTA   *(steadfast)* Please.

Life seeps into the lights, and sound brightens as we cross into:

Scene Sixteen

Isolate PAOLO.

PAOLO   *(warm and emotional)* A father builds a house for his family. That house is a symbol of him. It gives his family shelter and warmth and protects them from bad things—it keeps them in. A father starts building that house when he is still a child. When he sits and listens to his father speak—he starts with the first brick. While playing childhood games with his friends—he throws stones and bleeds at the lip to protect his land. As a young man, everything he does, every choice he makes is for the benefit of his family. Every dollar earned, first runs through the filter of the family, before he thinks of himself. They are him. What man is he without them? And one day, after his wife has brought forth his children—to carry on the name, and to support them in old age—he stands in front of a building and says: this is for you. Everything… *everything* is for them: that is a father.

Lights snap to black.

Scene Seventeen

Past. MARCO is in his room, changing out of his work clothes. He stands in his underwear, putting on his deodorant and cologne. We can hear the rest of the family downstairs in the middle of an animated storytelling. There is much laughter from the parents. MARCO notes this with a smile, he shakes his head in appreciation of his brother's ability. He begins dressing in his "going out" clothes. Audience acts as mirror. He sees GABRIEL, laughing as he walks by his door.

MARCO   Hey chump.

GABRIEL enters.

GABRIEL   Hey boss. Where are you going?

MARCO   Out. Meeting Dayna at the coffee shop.

GABRIEL   Cool. What pants are you gonna wear?

MARCO   Those ones.

GABRIEL   Ahh—your "nice jeans." With this shirt?

MARCO   Yeah, with that shirt. Hey, what were you saying downstairs?

GABRIEL   Nothing.

MARCO   Come on—they were pissing themselves.

GABRIEL   I was just fooling around, you know. I was imitating our aunt Carmela from last night. You know how she's all… *Woodbridge*.

MARCO   One word? That's it.

GABRIEL   That's all you need to describe her. Woodbridge. 'Nuff said.

They laugh.

MARCO   Pass my jeans. *(beat)* I can't believe how Pa's laughing, though.

GABRIEL   How come? He thinks it's funny, 'cause it's true.

MARCO   Yeah but, still, it's his sister…

GABRIEL   What, like he doesn't know she's high maintenance?

MARCO   Still, it doesn't mean he wants to watch his son doing impressions of her. I swear, you can get away with crazy shit, Gabe—it's funny.

GABRIEL   Oh please, he knows I'm just joking around. Holy, you're more uptight than he is—I hope you get some tonight.

                GABRIEL flops onto MARCO's bed.

MARCO   As if you'd know about getting any. Plus, I'm not uptight. Watch you don't wrinkle the—give me the shirt—careful.

GABRIEL   Easy there, stud. *(He passes him the shirt.)* You're worse than a girl.

                He turns onto his stomach on the bed (kitchen table), and grabs a porn magazine from under MARCO's clothes. He flips through it casually as the scene continues.

MARCO   All I'm saying is that I'm surprised to see him laughing—but then again, it is you we're talking about, so…

GABRIEL   What's that supposed to mean?

MARCO   You know you're probably the only one who can make him laugh like that. *(beat)* He thinks you're funny and so you get away with everything. With me? He breaks my balls for every fucking thing.

GABRIEL   Leave the shirt un-tucked—it looks better.

MARCO   Yeah?

GABRIEL   Trust me—only losers tuck their shirts into their jeans.

MARCO   I'll show you a loser. Don't get mouthy.

GABRIEL	Okayy, I'm just saying. *(beat)* But listen—about Pa; it's not that I'm really even funny, Mar— It's just that I include him.
MARCO	What the heck does that even mean: "I include him"—he lives here doesn't he?
GABRIEL	No, I mean that, just 'cause he's old-fashioned and everything, doesn't mean he wouldn't like to let loose and laugh. You know, be part of our normal… you know, conversations and shit.
MARCO	Okay, you're talking like a paralegal or something—what are you saying.
GABRIEL	Marco, it's like we treat him like the person he pretends to be—so he's always stuck being that person. See what I'm saying? He's never allowed to be anything else.

MARCO stops and looks at him, not understanding.

He was young once. I'm sure he liked to have fun and piss around with his friends.

MARCO	So?
GABRIEL	You know those black and white pictures of him—the ones of him when he was a young guy in Italy, before he had us?
MARCO	Yeah…
GABRIEL	—Where they're all wearing tight black sweaters and sunglasses, leaning on their Vespas? You know the ones.
MARCO	Yeah.
GABRIEL	Yeah, he's smiling and laughing in those photos.
MARCO	I know—there's that one where they're all on the beach in those stupid bathing suits, standing on each others shoulders in a pyramid.
GABRIEL	Exactly.
MARCO	So, what's your point?

GABRIEL   (*beat*) He's beautiful in those pictures.

MARCO   Easy now, beautiful…

GABRIEL   Mar, don't be retarded, you know what I mean.

MARCO   Whatever, yeah, he was a good-looking guy back then.

GABRIEL   More than that, though. (*beat*) He was looser, happier. But all that is still in him somewhere.

MARCO   I guess.

GABRIEL   He's a human being, Mar.

MARCO   (*sarcastic*) Oh really?

GABRIEL   Yeah. But maybe you forget that. Wanna know what I do sometimes? (*beat*) I look at him and I squint my eyes.

MARCO   You're a nut.

GABRIEL   Seriously. When I squint, it smoothes out all the lines—and he looks like his pictures again. Young.

MARCO   Seriously man, you're a goof.

GABRIEL   Try it, Mar—it might make you talk to him differently. You and Ma talk to him in a way that he can't just be a person—he always has to have the answer with you both. It's never a conversation.

MARCO   What? (*recognizing it as true*) Please, that is such crap …pshh.

GABRIEL   Fine, whatever… you know I'm talking truth here, that's why it bugs you.

MARCO   Okay, Gabe, you're breaking my balls, now.

GABRIEL   For real though, could you imagine what it must be like for him. Go to work, come home—and entire days go by without any real connection? Not from your employees, not from your family for godsake. Day in, day out—no wonder he's crusty.

MARCO	Okay great, I'm a bad, bad son—I'm so mean. Cool. So what? What are we even talking about already?
GABRIEL	*(re: PAOLO)* I think it's the saddest thing.
MARCO	Look, I'm sorry and everything—but he chose to be that way. And so now everyone treats him like that. I love him and everything—he's my father, but he's a hard person, Gabe. That's the way he wanted it… sorry, but that's what I think.
GABRIEL	*(with a defeated air)* It's even sadder that you think someone would choose to be that way.
MARCO	*(pause)* Anyhow, all I was trying to say is that it's good that you make him laugh. You make everyone laugh 'cause you're a dumbass.
GABRIEL	*(flattered)* Shut up.
MARCO	—But, whatever… it's all good. That's your, a, talent. In case you were looking for one—that's what it is: You're funny. Okay? Now shut up—I gotta get ready.
GABRIEL	*(imitating his brother's butch-macho-voice)* Oh yah? Well okay then—cool.
MARCO	Are you done?
GABRIEL	Yup.

> *MARCO playfully gives him a light punch to the shoulder.*

	Do you think it's possible to put any more cologne on?
MARCO	Ha-ha-ha. Hilarious. *(beat)* Well, I guess you're gonna be happy then, cause it looks like us three are gonna be spending a lot of "quality time" together, starting this weekend. Pa's decided that we're gonna start finishing the basement.
GABRIEL	*(crestfallen)* …What.

MARCO	Yup: you, me and Pops. He finally decided to finish it—he wants to have all the relatives over for Christmas Eve this year, in the new basement.
GABRIEL	You're serious.
MARCO	Um, yeah, he's ordered the drywall and shit already—I had to get three boxes of finishing nails. *(beat)* Why do you look so surprised? You knew we were gonna have to do it eventually. When he gets something in his head, there's no way around it.
GABRIEL	I know.
MARCO	Let's go eat, I'm parched.

MARCO exits.

GABRIEL stands locked for a second, then follows. The lights are drained of past life, and sound transitions us into:

Scene Eighteen

PAOLO walks toward the centre of the floor level. He walks very slowly with an energy that is heavy, bound, and sustained. When he reaches the centre point, he stops, turns his back to the audience, and looks up at the dimensions of the room, and then stares straight ahead blankly. His plan is useless.

Cross into:

Scene Nineteen

MATT and GABRIEL appear on the bridge. A week after we last saw them. Winter has taken hold. GABRIEL holds MATT's skateboard. They stand very close to each other. They are both holding on to a lot of emotion. They stare at each other. MATT seems invested in a way that is overwhelming to them both. Both are trying to keep from crying. Neither one wants to be the first to leave.

Silence.

MATT   Gabe, look, I'm sorry.

GABRIEL   Matt... don't... please.

Uncomfortable pause.

MATT   They want my dad to start by the new year, so they want him relocated before the holidays even. I didn't know they already had a place for us and everything. *(beat)* So... yeah.

GABRIEL   ...Okay.

MATT   Okay, so... so, I gotta to go now. I have to. My parents're waiting.

GABRIEL   I know. Okay.

MATT   Okay, all right, so...

GABRIEL   ...I can't believe all of this is happening at once.

MATT   Gabe, come on look, this isn't the big move yet, you know—that won't happen for a few more weeks. We'll be back on Monday, we're just dropping off the storage boxes for now—that's all. *(beat)* I'm coming back.

GABRIEL   For what, a week? Two? Then what? You're moving away, Matt—that's what's happening. You're leaving.

MATT   *(Beat. He releases a frustrated sigh, that unleashes his anger.)* I know, I know, I know—This is so STUPID. You know what?—I hate my Dad, I hate him and his stupid job—I hate always having to move ...I hate this. *(beat)* Gabe, I don't want to move this time; I don't want to leave you.

GABRIEL   Please stop saying that... It won't change anything.

GABRIEL looks away, he's about to lose it.

MATT   Gabriel. *(beat)* Look at me.

GABRIEL   I can't.

Pause.

MATT So what, you're just not gonna say anything?

GABRIEL What do you want me to say, Matt? This is what you do, right? You said it yourself; you're never in the same place for long—"Them the breaks," right?

MATT Yeah but that was before.

GABRIEL Before what …?

MATT You know, before *us*. *(beat)* Before everything we did together—imagined together. Before we laid out in the field behind our—

GABRIEL Matt can you stop?! *Holy*. You made it up, okay?! There was no field. There *is* no field—None of it exists, and now—

MATT What the hell is that?! Gabe look, listen to me; I wasn't playing around with you—it wasn't just sex. It was us together… our first time together—don't make it sound like a game. It was beautiful and real—and you know that. *(beat)* Why are you being like this to me?

GABRIEL Why? Because I seem to be the only one dealing with reality here. *(beat)* You have no clue what I'm in right now, Matt.

MATT I'm trying, Gabe, but you're shutting down on me. Talk to me.

GABRIEL *(beat)* For the past week my father has been working on the basement—finishing it. Do you understand what that means?

MATT What do you mean?

GABRIEL It'll be done, soon. "Our little kitchen" will be finished. What then?

MATT Gabe, you never said anything—

GABRIEL He's split it into two rooms. Even the sink is in place, Matt. Remember… the pipe for the sink?—well, it's in now.

MATT	Why didn't you tell me this was happening? *(beat)* WHY?
GABRIEL	*(starts to cry)* He split it into two rooms. Our imaginary "home" is gone—and that's just beginning.
MATT	Gabe, I don't understand, why would you keep this from me?—We tell each other everything—
GABRIEL	Because, Matt. I wanted to pretend it wasn't happening—don't you see? As long as you're here, I can pretend, but when you go, what am I gonna do?
MATT	We shouldn't have to pretend anything. I fucking hate this shit. Fuck.
GABRIEL	Matt, I'm really scared, okay—
MATT	—I know, me too—but, please Gabe, don't pretend like it never happened. Do you hear me? It'll be okay—
GABRIEL	It's NOT going to be okay—all right?! I'm gonna be ALONE.
MATT	—Well what do you want me to say: FINE, we'll both be alone—*together*. *(beat)* Christ, this isn't going good, is it.

Pause. They both realize they don't want to be arguing, and so, proceed with renewed care and honesty.

GABRIEL	I don't know how to do this. I don't know how to go back to how it was before; *hiding*—what am I supposed to do? Matt, honestly, how's this ever supposed to work?
MATT	We'll figure something out—*I* will figure it out, okay? But, please— *(beat)* I never faked anything with you, okay? All of it was real. I'm not sorry I met you—Gabriel? I'm not; I don't regret anything; we found something. Look at me. Listen, what we have is fucking gold—and if no one else gets it— fuck 'em. Do you hear me? *Gold. (beat)* And... well... that's all. *(smiling)* So... shut up.

GABRIEL takes his face and kisses him tenderly on the lips. MATT is a bit thrown off and tense.

(referring to potential witnesses) Gabe—there's people…

GABRIEL   I don't care anymore.

They both give over to an unapologetically, full, emotional embrace.

MATT   This isn't goodbye I told you—look at me—I'm coming back on Monday, and we don't move till the 14th—so we still have time left, even if it's shorter than we thought.

GABRIEL   *(suddenly very sad)* Matt… why do I feel like everything's ending?

MATT   *(weakly)* Gabe… please.

MATT starts to cry. GABRIEL hugs him harder.

GABRIEL   Shh, it's okay… it's not your fault.

GABRIEL slowly releases him

I don't want you to get in shit. *(beat)* You should go.

MATT   I have to. *(beat)* So we're good, we're cool?

GABRIEL   *(trying to put on a brave face)* Yup. *(beat)* We're cool.

MATT   Okay… So, I'll see you when I get back.

He turns to leave.

GABRIEL   Matt …you should take this.

GABRIEL holds out his skateboard.

MATT   Oh. Right. Thanks.

He crosses to GABRIEL, and takes the board. He lingers.

Thank you.

Silence.

	Please don't be sad. It won't change anything.
GABRIEL	I know, it won't. *(beat)* You'd better get going.
MATT	*(beat)* I need you to know one thing… I really think, you and me—the two of us; what we have is… *(pause)* Never mind. it's okay—I should just shut up: I'm only making this harder for both of us.
GABRIEL	Tell me.
MATT	What good will it do?
GABRIEL	Matt, what were you gonna say?
MATT	Gabe, come on. *(beat)* You already know. *(beat)* I see your eyes—you *know* what this is, we're feeling.
GABRIEL	*(desperately sad)* Let me hear you say it, Matthew—just once, out loud—and then who knows?… Maybe…?
MATT	I… *(beat)* I have to go now.
	Silence.
GABRIEL	Me too.

> MATT gives GABRIEL one final kiss without an embrace. MATT holds for a second, he's about to say "I love you," but then backs up and runs off, leaving GABRIEL in stunned sadness.

NB: From this point on the remaining scenes will play out without clearing the participants of the prior scenes. Each scene will play, while the other characters maintain their final positions of the previous scene.

Scene Twenty

> Upstairs kitchen dining table. Four plate settings. As GABRIEL makes his way into the scene, the other actors stand in their places facing upstage in a neutral state of stillness—only when GABRIEL has taken his position do they snap into the scene. PAOLO sits at one end, he has pushed away from his setting. CONCETTA, having removed GABRIEL's

coat and seating him, is herself seated at the other end of the table. GABRIEL sits at the upstage centre position, facing out to the audience—transfixed on something they can't see: MATT who now stands in the audience with his back turned. MARCO has pushed away from his place and stands with a napkin in his collar in the upstage corner. He paces tightly.

They are silent, save for their breath—or lack thereof.

MARCO   No... Gabriel. No. NO—I don't think you know what you're saying here: trying to say. What are you trying to say...?

No response.

THIS is not the time to be quiet, okay?! *(to PAOLO)* Pa? Pa, I don't think he, um, understands what he said, okay? So... he's not saying it right.
I don't think.

No response. MARCO crouches beside GABRIEL.

What are you doing? Huh? Do you have any idea of the mess you're starting? Take it back! *(grabbing GABRIEL and shaking him)* YOU NEED TO TAKE IT BACK, YOU LITTLE—

CONCETTA   / MARCO!!

PAOLO   / ENOUGH!!

CONCETTA pulls MARCO off, and takes him upstage. They all try to breathe.

(with an eerie calm) No more of this. *(beat)* No more. Enough. I know what has happened here—and now I am stopping everything. Too many liberties—and now enough.

CONCETTA   *(returning to the table)* Paolo, drink the water... shhh. Nothing has happened—there is no need for nothing. Marco sit. We all need to stop talking. Just eat... I made the food—I MADE THE FOOD... Please.

PAOLO clears half the table in one swipe, sending everything crashing onto the floor.

PAOLO!! NO!

She immediately starts collecting the debris and placing it in the tablecloth.

PAOLO Concetta. /

CONCETTA Paolo, please. You make a mess for nothing, / please…

PAOLO Sit down. /

CONCETTA Why can't we all just pretend— /

PAOLO SIT DOWN! SIT!!

She does. He locks his eyes onto GABRIEL. He leans into him, and speaks calmly. He continues speaking throughout the next several sections, not stopping for the others' interjections. He is unwavering in his need to clarify.

Gabriele, look just at me, no one else. Listen good… I don't know why, but you have brought this into my house, and you will remove it. Okay? *(beat)* You can not think that with a few words, you are going to be allowed to destroy everything that I have worked for.

MARCO Pa, he doesn't realize what he said / —he didn't mean it—

PAOLO *(to GABRIEL)* YOU! You will not rob me of my family. You will not destroy our peace, Gabriele. It's not allowed. *(beat)* You are the youngest—the hope! The youngest is supposed to be the walking cane of the parents in their old age—but you do THIS? You walk in here, and, and—you're a LIAR!! / You lied to me about everything!

CONCETTA —Please stop! We can not say these things. Paolo—

PAOLO   I sat with you. I talked with you. I asked you about your life, so I could be closer to you—but you told me NOTHING! You said nothing. You lied to me, Gabriele, about who you are.

> *A long pause, in which he tries to keep from crying.*

That is finished now. *(to GABRIEL)* You want us to "accept?" Accept. There is nothing to accept— DO YOU UNDERSTAND!? I will not accept that with a PIG choice, that YOU are gonna decide what is acceptable now—In my house?! In my family?! With my NAME!? My poor father's name—and you just, you make UNCLEAN my father's name like a, a—/

CONCETTA   PAOLO!! / *Per favore, basta!*

MARCO   / Pa, don't this—*Pa!*

> *MARCO and CONCETTA continue pleading throughout PAOLO's following lines—building almost a wall of sound—until he yells at them specifically in his second section.*

PAOLO   You have never had to protect anything—ANYTHING! What would you ever understand about honour or, or, or *obligation*? Huh? ANSWER ME, GODAMMIT! *(beat)* We do things for to help the family, not for ourselves—how many things, HOW MANY THINGS have I never done because all of you were in front of my head—burned into my eyes. But for *you* there is no consideration of *us*— we're nothing to you. /

CONCETTA   God in heaven… /

MARCO   / Can we please stop this, / PLEASE!

CONCETTA   /Holy Mary…

PAOLO   *(to GABRIEL)* / I want you to understand one thing. In my day, do you know what they would have—*(to the others)* Everyone SHUT UP!! *(pause)* I want him to understand who *I* am. *(back to*

	GABRIEL) Gabriele, back then, if someone did what you… do… they would have put a burlap sack over that boy's head and tied it shut around his neck with his own father's belt—Do you understand what I'm saying to you? THIS is where I come from—understand? Those people would tighten the sack around that boy's head, and they would take him in the night, to the outskirts of a town, and they would throw him down an abandoned well!
MARCO	Okay, enough! He gets it. What is wrong with us—just STOP!
PAOLO	NO. No. Someone's got to understand the way I was taught to deal with things. Someone must understand that everything is NOT like the TV. There are very bad and complete ends to certain things… what is the word—CONSEQUENCE. Someone needs to understand that I am not the bad man here. I am sparing you, Gabriele: Because of my own mistakes with you, because of where I raised you—I spare you. *I* am to blame for this… *wandering.* (beat) But, when you think that I am terrible man without a heart—just remember what I have explained to you about other fathers.

> *Silence. PAOLO swiftly pulls his chair near to GABRIEL—the others gasp, expecting violence. PAOLO speaks quietly in GABRIEL's ear.*

Gabriele, it is very difficult—but it is very simple; I am not going to acknowledge this. Ever. So, find a way to get this out of you. I don't want to know, just do whatever you need to. There is nothing for anyone outside this house to know about, because nothing has changed. This will never be spoken about again. I have not thrown you out in the street—I would never do that. You were mistaken and I forgive you. *(beat)* Go fix yourself. Life is hard enough as it is, without you making it harder for you, for everyone. *Please.* Go wash.

> PAOLO *gets up. Deflated yet steadfast. He looks at each of them before leaving. Silence.*

MARCO Everything is gonna be okay. Okay?... just shake it off, and move on as if nothing happened. *(beat)* He's giving you another chance, Gabe. Just do it. He is right you know—life is hard enough.

CONCETTA *(shell-shocked)* Marco shut your mouth for me. How are we ever going to sit at this table again and keep the food down.

> *She gets up unsteadily and makes as if to continue clearing the mess.*

MARCO Ma. Ma, please, just go do—don't worry about the mess right now. Go sit down somewhere. I'll clean this, don't worry.

> *He turns her to face him.*

Ma, just... go. It's okay. Go.

> CONCETTA *in her state, takes forever to leave in the same direction* PAOLO *went.* MARCO *waits until she is finally gone before turning to* GABRIEL. *He sits in the chair that was pulled up beside* GABRIEL. MARCO, *slowly shakes his head. Finally:*

I don't really, um... shit, Gabe. What the hell ever made you think you could... in *this* family? Who the hell are you? Huh? What were you thinking? What world do you live in?

> MARCO *looks at him a long time, realizes he isn't actually waiting for an answer, and begins gathering up the mess. He replaces* PAOLO's *chair. He leaves without looking at* GABRIEL.
>
> GABRIEL *alone.*
>
> *He still faces out in the direction of* MATT.
>
> MATT *very suddenly walks away.*
>
> GABRIEL's *eyes re-focus, and with it comes a wave of reality. Gravity. He remains seated, looking out,*

as the next scene plays out near the apron of the stage.

Scene Twenty-one

MUSIC transitions us into the basement mid-construction. PAOLO stands leaning against one of the 2x4 walls—it seemingly holds him up. He covers his eyes and forehead with one hand, while smoking with the other—it is his first cigarette in years. He checks up at the reality of the construction and looks back at his hands. He extinguishes his cigarette and spits.

PAOLO …God…

He turns around and begins slowly banging his forehead into the lumber he was leaning against. He holds onto his head and stops. His shoulders betray that he is weeping silently. At the opposite side of the stage, CONCETTA has been watching the latter part of this, from the dark. She steps into the space, her eyes wet. She crosses and attempts to console her husband. Carefully, she approaches him and stands near him—not knowing what to do, exactly.

CONCETTA Paolo? *Caro?* What are we gonna do?

He turns on her. He is seething.

PAOLO "What are we going to do?" Hm. What are we going to do—she asks me. First thing is: you're going to leave him to me—he is not your daughter.

CONCETTA looks as though she's been slapped.

CONCETTA You blame me…?

PAOLO I blame no one but myself. I strayed from the plan, Concetta. There is a reason why the old way of raising them works—and that is: because it *works*. If freedom is not earned Concetta—this is what happens.

CONCETTA I don't know how you are speaking right now, Paolo? Don't be like this—

She goes to caress him. He moves away from her.

PAOLO Don't.

She is stunned, as he begins to walk towards the direction she entered from.

CONCETTA Paolo, we have to be together on this—that is the only way it can work. *(beat)* Paolo, he comes from us.

This stops him. He turns to face her.

PAOLO Concetta. *(beat)* Be quiet.

CONCETTA Who are you right now?

PAOLO I am who I have to be.

He turns away from her and leaves. CONCETTA is left standing with a hand covering her mouth, the other absently picking at her apron; she looks abnormally young, and remarkably old at the same time. After a moment she removes her apron, and throws it on the ground. Meanwhile MARCO has entered in the background and is laying out plates of pasta at each setting at that kitchen table. PAOLO enters and stands beside his seat. In unison, he and MARCO take their seats. CONCETTA slowly turns and makes her way to her seat, she stands beside her seat for a beat, then sits. The lights shift to convey a change in time.

Scene Twenty-two

Three days after the "coming out" in Scene Twenty. The upstairs kitchen dining table. Supper. The tension that remains from the "revelation" boils underneath the forced exterior. The family sits in their respective places. GABRIEL is obscured on and off by MARCO, sitting directly across from

	him. *Everyone has one eye on their food, and the other on each other—except for GABRIEL, who listlessly brings food to his mouth. His brain is overflowing with too many thoughts. The men speak with a forced focus, while CONCETTA speaks without being acknowledged. The punctuation before her lines indicates that she doesn't receive audience in the pacing of the scene, but she is not overlapped by the others.*
MARCO	*(to PAOLO)* ...yeah, well that's what *I* said. *(beat)* I mean really, either way you're set: tax or no tax. I mean you could live off the interest alone, and you would still be... you know. I mean you could actually live off the interest and be set. That is some crazy money. Seriously, it's ...a lot.
PAOLO	Well, that's *other* people, no? If you sit around waiting for luck like that, you won't ever leave the house. It's best not to think about it.
CONCETTA	–That's right. No.
MARCO	No, I know—I'm just saying... could you imagine, though?
PAOLO	That's why at work, these people on the lines sew their fingers into the lining; because they got one eye on the work in front of them, and the other is too busy dreaming of Hawaii.
CONCETTA	–Luck happens good, and bad: someone wins a million dollars and two houses down someone gets cancer. *(She immediately knocks three times on the table.)*
PAOLO	There are people in the world who will go to their graves without ever even being able to see a postcard of Hawaii. What is Hawaii to these people?
CONCETTA	–It's better to have no luck at all, good or bad. No luck. I hate this word.
MARCO	Ma, what are you talking about, even? Pa's saying something here.

PAOLO   Forget Hawaii, and work. Work. That's what you should pay attention to. At the end of the day, you know, *it* is what will save you—not waiting for luck.

MARCO   Hawaii.

PAOLO   It's not a paradise. It's just a place.

MARCO   No, yeah, you're completely right, Pa. 'Cause, some—I don't know, tourism guy decided: "yeah I'll sell it as paradise, and then people will... whatever." You're completely right—It's true.

CONCETTA   –A million people a year must die just trying to get to Hawaii.

               Beat. Silence. Eating.

PAOLO   Paradise?... Sometimes I seen paradise going north on the 400—it don't matter. Maybe just the bend on the highway, and the way the rock... wall... just appears out of nowhere. Flat land— then all at once you look up ahead and it's big, big granite rock shining in the sun.

               They all ponder the moment. Silence. Eating.

CONCETTA   When I am alone, sometimes I see the birds outside the window and I think... no. *(beat)* At the grocery store, sometimes I see paradise; when the, when I look at the beautiful tomatoes all piled up, and then out of nowhere the water starts misting on them... and I can see my face in the mirror wall behind them, and it looks like I'm a giant. My face is the sky, the tomatoes are the red hills, and there is the nice rain washing everything away. That is paradise.

               GABRIEL turns and smiles warmly at his mother. She meets his eyes. Collective beat. She turns away, afraid to hold the connection. Beat.

PAOLO   *(to MARCO)* So is he going to get someone to manage the money for him?

MARCO What, like a, a financial guy? Finances guy?

PAOLO No, I think a money manager—or whatever they are called: a man to watch his money.

MARCO Right, oh yeah, like a financial manager. Yeah, he's getting one. I think. Well, he should, right?…

PAOLO I don't know. I would.

He gets up and begins to exit. MARCO follows right behind.

MARCO Oh yeah, completely. *I* would definitely… yup.

The two men are gone. Beat.

CONCETTA slowly rises and begins making her way around the table clearing the plates. She speaks as she does this. Not directly to GABRIEL, but for him.

CONCETTA Outside is so many birds, you know. Flying …flying wherever they want to. That is the only real paradise. Everything else is a cage. The tamed birds can only *sing* of freedom, but wild birds… they actually fly.

She hesitates before leaving the stage. GABRIEL is still. After a moment he slowly makes his way up to standing, and crosses downstage to the apron of the stage. PAOLO has walked on from the wings to take his position beside, but at a distance from GABRIEL. As they arrive at their spots in unison the lights shift to: a dark stage with two isolated shafts of light over both men, as they stand still facing out.

Scene Twenty-three

A split scene. Two spotlights over both actors, isolate each, and create two distinct locations. Simultaneously PAOLO and GABRIEL prepare for sleep. They undress down to their undergarments as they speak. (GABRIEL gets down to his white hip-briefs. PAOLO gets down to an undershirt and briefs.) Methodically they remove each article of clothing. PAOLO as if praying for guidance.

>   GABRIEL *as in a silent conversation, looking for*
>   *confirmation.*

PAOLO   A father who loves his son will confine him. *(beat)*
                If a son is disciplined, he will be of some use, and
                his father can boast of him to his friends. While
                the father is alive, the sight of his son makes him
                happy, and when he dies, he has no regrets. He is
                not really dead, because his son is like him. ...This
                is the only way.

GABRIEL   This is the only way. *(beat)* There is nothing to be
                afraid of.

>   PAOLO *walks out of the light as if heading to bed.*
>   GABRIEL *stands for a long time staring out*
>   *blankly, before exiting in the opposite direction of*
>   *his father.*

Scene Twenty-four

>   *Lights rise to reveal* MARCO *and* CONCETTA *on*
>   *top of the kitchen table, as they ended Scene Fifteen.*
>   *They continue from where they left off in that earlier,*
>   *present scene.* MARCO *has moved away from*
>   CONCETTA *in an attempt to galvanize himself.*
>   *She looks at him intensely—with equal parts expec-*
>   *tation and fear. He begins with trepidation.*

MARCO   I knew something was wrong the second I came
                in the front door, that day. I could feel it. *(beat)*
                I could feel it, Ma. I called out your name, even
                though I knew you were out doing groceries.
                I took off my shoes— 'cause it had snowed. I took
                off my coat, and I went into the kitchen. I saw
                Gabriel's schoolbag hanging off the coat thing.
                I called out his name—but there was no response.
                Nothing. He'd gone to school without his bag.
                I remember noticing that the house was freezing
                cold. I went into the front room and checked the
                temperature—but it was at 20, which didn't make
                sense with how cold I felt. *(beat)* Something wasn't

	right. All at once, I got really freaked out. I remember, I stopped moving. I stood still and just listened—like as if there might actually be a thief or someone in the house.
CONCETTA	Marco. *(gently)* Tell me.

> *MARCO focuses and starts replaying the events in his mind. At times, he seems to be "reporting" the facts, rather than re-experiencing them. Other times he is thrown back, wildly, into the events.*

MARCO	*(beat)* I hadn't noticed it when I came in, but—all at once, my eyes went straight to it… the note on the phone desk. "Marco." I opened it—his writing: "Marco, I'm sorry. Call the police. Don't come downstairs. This is the only way. I'm not afraid. I'm sorry. I love you all, Gabriel." Oh Ma, please…
CONCETTA	–Speak.
MARCO	*(He barrels through.)* My whole body just filled up like a, a—and I was flying down the basement stairs screaming his name—screaming GABRIEL and crying hot. Into the card room—empty, nothing. No. I run, I run into the kitchen, Ma. And the heat in there. The basement kitchen—There he is… I drop to my knees and I puke everything.

> *CONCETTA covers her mouth, muttering "God… God" throughout.*

I'm throwing up very hard, Ma, so's I can feel something pop in my eye. *(pause)* I look up at him. I look at my brother, my… it's Gabe, Ma… Gabriel, hanging from the beam. Naked. My heart is in my mouth—my lungs… above me, like on meat-hooks; every breath kills me. I feel like I'm seriously drowning—cement pouring into my ears. *(beat)* Gabriel. I keep blinking, blinking—blinking crazy like, like if I keep shutting what I'm seeing maybe—when I look again it won't be real—WHAT am I seeing—GOD—my baby brother… oh God, God,

God, God, God God God GOD GOD GOD God
God God... God... what have you done?

> MARCO *stands as if he can't catch his breath. He holds his head.* CONCETTA *slowly curls up as small as she can, still on her knees, still on top of the table.* MARCO *focuses again and continues.*

The basement kitchen, Ma. *(beat)* The only uncovered beam we had left to drywall. He tied a rope around it. And now there was nothing I could do. *(beat)* He was so still. That was what killed me; seeing him... so still. His eyes were already empty; glass. *(beat)* He wasn't scary, Ma—if that's what you were thinking—he was *beautiful*. A statue... all handsome, and still, and tight. He looked like that saint—the young man... Saint Thomas, or no, no—Sebastian, Saint... *(beat)* He wasn't ours no more, Ma. That was it. He was gone. *(beat)* There was a heat around him. *Heat*; like a humidity almost—but just around his body. I got up. I was dripping with sweat, puke, my crying. I held my hands up to him, like I was warming my hands near a fire—how stupid is that? But it was *his* heat. I breathed in his heat 'cause it was all that was left of him being alive— I did it. I wrapped my stupid arms around his legs. I lifted him—so's I could carry his weight. My face against his thigh, I held onto him tight and I spoke to him quietly, like it was just the two of us—like always. I spoke for a long time. Sometimes I ran out of stuff to say to him, and then I would just listen to the traffic on the street outside. I could hear the cars on the street through the basement window—just going on like normal. That had been me only an hour before—but it would never be me again. People... just driving. I said to Gabe; those people have no idea what you've gone and done. No idea.

> MARCO *begins to weep. He covers his face.* CONCETTA *sits up and rests her head on his leg,*

comforts him. He lowers and rests his head on her lap as she clears his hair away from his face. She looks as though she'd just crawled out of the rubble from a bombing. She gives him a moment.

CONCETTA   What are *not* you telling me?

MARCO   What…?

CONCETTA   What else? *(beat)* I know you, Marco. There is something you are not saying.

Lights shift, dropping out on the kitchen table, and slowly coming up on the periphery of the set to reveal:

Scene Twenty-five

GABRIEL is dressed only in white hip-briefs. He is soaked from head to toe. He rubs his arms against cold. He is slowly walking alongside the walls of the room. He is faintly lit, almost glowing.

GABRIEL   You can walk in a circle your whole life. You can do this, and never once dare to look at what it is you're circling. And maybe you can be happy like this, because you can look out, and see that all around you everyone's doing the same. You can look past them and see even more people walking in circles—and maybe this makes you feel safe, because you are obviously doing what you're supposed to be doing. Look at them all. Nothing's wrong. Millions of people, millions of blind circles; like, if you were able to float up, high above yourself—I mean *so* high up, that it's freezing cold—and if you could look down on everything below, you would see the whole blue world covered with tiny people walking in circles; like some giant Olympic opening ceremony …or something… *(beat)* I'm walking my same old circle. I'm looking out, never in—always out. And something is… something feels different; not good or bad, just, like whatever it is, is happening on its own.

All at once, everything around me starts shifting, changing. All the circling people are starting to fade—not disappear or anything, but just fade; like a picture that's been left in a window for years; there, but not clear anymore. Nothing else is either, anymore; clear. I'm breathing higher and quicker. I don't really know what's happening to me—but it is happening. I'm small. Fragile. I am permeable. My skin is... I am... *(beat)* So—so I keep my eyes shut tight against it all. I just keep walking my circle—'cause that's what I know, right? Right?! Walk in a circle. Walk in a circle. It's not the same anymore... walk in a... circle. *(beat)* I smell something; incredible.

> GABRIEL *begins making his way towards downstage centre in front of the kitchen table.*

Not a smell, no—more of a scent—yes, like the incense in church; flowers and sweat. Oh God *oh God*—it comes in through my skin now; it fills me. I take up so much more space. I'm walking slower now—steps. I breathe slower—I'm all right. *(beat)* The scent comes from the centre.

> GABRIEL *is now standing downstage centre facing out. He is standing in warm glow.* MATT *appears on the bridge, standing centre looking out. He looks straight ahead—never once at* GABRIEL.

I stop. Every thought, every worry, every wish—everything stops. This amazing scent comes from the centre of the circle I've been walking this whole time. *(beat)* I turn to see. I face the centre of my circle. *(beat)* THERE—right there—in the centre—standing; the most beautiful thing I've ever seen. And it is... him. *(beat)* He looks at me without holding anything back. He looks at me fully—his eyes want to... my eyes, my face is like *art* to him. My knees are... gone. *(beat)* I have never been beautiful to anyone before. *(beat)* I take up so much space. I move into what used to be my circle—finally breathing makes sense. I walk towards him. His eyes don't let go of me; green like the bottom of an August lake—a smile built into the corners. At me—I am what he's looking at. *(beat)* I get it, finally: I was in the centre of his circle. Perfect. He stands so close, that my eyes blur—close your eyes. He puts his face into my neck—warm breath spreads across my skin. Neither of us knows a thing. We just stand there, our bodies learn each other—separate from our brains. My head spins. The two of us breathe the same. I can't smell that amazing scent anymore—and I finally understand; I can't smell it anymore because I've *tasted* it—it lives on the inside of his bottom lip, and it feels like… heaven.

> *Lights slowly pulse and dim, as GABRIEL and MATT both stand with closed eyes, as if with the other. After a beat GABRIEL slowly takes a step forward as the lights surge up to a blinding brightness, before going black.*
>
> *Beat. The kitchen table lights surge up on the prior scene. GABRIEL and MATT are gone.*

Scene Twenty-six

> *Lights return to their prior setting, on MARCO and CONCETTA, in their last position on top of the table. They speak at a break-neck intensity.*

CONCETTA What else. *(beat)* Tell me what you have to. I'm doing what you wanted. You told me that I have to accept the truth—but I need to hear it first. I want to know everything.

MARCO I told you.

CONCETTA The truth. The TRUTH. *(beat)* MARCO, I want to know what you did after you found him. How did you get back upstairs? How long were you there before—

MARCO   Please don't make me do this.

CONCETTA   You opened this—*you* did—and now you close it. *(beat)* Your father said he found you upstairs near the bedrooms. You were sitting in the bathroom. Tell me why. *(beat)* WHY?!—

MARCO   BECAUSE! Goddamnit! Because I didn't know where to go—I didn't know anything... *Please.*

> *CONCETTA's eyes are locked on him, she will wait forever for him to answer if she needs to.*

(weakly) Please.

CONCETTA   Tell me, and then maybe finally this nightmare will be over. *(beat)* Give me something real. *(beat)* Please.

> *MARCO, eyes-averted, half mumbles to himself.*

MARCO   "Give you something?" ...give you something.

> *MARCO forces himself to look her in the eyes.*

Everything, then.

> *CONCETTA nods.*

(beat) The rosary. *(pause)* How I found his rosary— That's what I never told you about.

CONCETTA   What rosary? What are you talking about?

MARCO   *(beat)* Gabriel's rosary. *(beat)* How do you have it? ...I thought it was buried with him.

> *CONCETTA takes it out.*

CONCETTA   This? His rosary? What do you mean, *how* do I have it?

> *CONCETTA seems to begin locking up internally.*

(cold) It was in his room. Where he keeps it.

MARCO   *(horrified by the error)* No... *No*, Ma. That's not right. It was supposed to be buried with him. That's what he wanted. I told Pa to put it in the coffin. I told him to do that.

CONCETTA …Marco?

MARCO *(It dawns on him.)* Pa didn't do it—He never gave it to the guy to put in the coffin! The lid was closed—I didn't know.

CONCETTA What are you talking about!?

MARCO Ma. Gabriel wanted to be buried with that rosary.

> *Pause. CONCETTA begins to take in too much air.*

CONCETTA No—how—what…

> *CONCETTA cannot compute what she's hearing.*

MARCO Ma, just—look: When we were little you taught us that wearing the rosary was sacrilegious, right?—Do you remember why?

CONCETTA …why what…

MARCO His rosary—the day you bought it for his First Communion, remember? He took it out of the box and wore it around his neck—and you freaked out. You yelled at him to take it off, "It's a sin to wear a rosary. Never wear the rosary!"

CONCETTA It is a sin—I didn't lie.

MARCO Do you remember what Gabe said, before he took it off? He looked like he was about to cry. He asked you, "How can it be a sin if it comes from God?" And you couldn't answer him. No one could. Because he was right.

CONCETTA What does his rosary have to do with the truth? Why… the… ros—

> *She grabs her chest as if it has been kicked with the slow realization.*

Oh God. Why are you telling me, Marco. NO, no this rosary was in its box in his bedroom. What are you saying?

MARCO That rosary you're holding was there when he died, Ma.

CONCETTA (beat) No. Where was it?... No. NO.

> MARCO stands. CONCETTA disintegrates. Keening.

MARCO It was on him—I'm sorry. (beat) He was wearing it.

CONCETTA (She is covering her eyes.) I'm not HERE—MARCO STOP TALKING MARCO PLEEEEASE.

> CONCETTA breathes heavy. She slowly moves her hands, but is still shielding her eyes, as if from an impending explosion. MARCO takes this as a cue to continue.

MARCO (beat) I was going to take him down—and, that's when I saw it. Under the rope. Like a— /

CONCETTA (weakly keening the confirmation of the image) AYII...NOOO... / NOOOO ... Perche, Gabriele? Gabriele... Mio povero figlio, perche? (Why, Gabriele? Gabriele... My poor son, why?)

MARCO / Yes. He was wearing it like a necklace, under the rope. (beat) At first I didn't understand—on top of everything, why would he have done THAT. Why? I didn't get it, Ma. Why? WHY?!
I looked at him and thought: YOU GABRIEL NO. (beat) Oh God, Ma—I got so so mad. Whatever I had left; I lost it. I started yelling—hitting myself—yelling at him: YOU stupid fucker! You stupid *stupid* idiot—HOW could you do this?! What are you thinking?!—This is nobody else's fault, GODAMMN you—this is ALL you! You did this! YOU did this!!... You stupid Gabriel, Gabriel, Gabriel come back RIGHT NOW!!! (pause) I ripped that rosary off his neck—I didn't care. I turned away from him and went all the way up the stairs to the bedroom floor. Yes. I stood outside his room with his rosary in my hand. Okay? I went down on my knees, Ma, and I reconnected the beads with my teeth—'cause I'd broken it—that's what I did. I got up. I walked into his room. I didn't look at nothing. No. I didn't want to touch

anything—I went over to his nightstand. Right?
There was the little blue case. I put the rosary back
in it. Yes, that's what I did. I did all those things.
(beat) I tried to save you, Ma. That's why I did
that. *(beat)* I couldn't save him, but I tried to save
you. *(pause)*

> CONCETTA *turns over on her back and lays flat
> across the kitchen table, she is spent. Her rib-cage
> heaves with grief.*

I was standing in his room, for a second, it was
kinda like I'd blacked out, but with my eyes open.
Then I remembered where I was. I turned, to go,
and I saw—on his bed, he'd... laid out his good
suit... the suit for the coffin. *(beat)* See, Ma? That
was when I understood why he was wearing the
rosary: If he was from God, then how could he be
wrong? That was the message... He wore the
rosary when he died because he wanted to be
buried like that... God around his neck. *(beat)* In
his head, he knew what he was doing. He was
never stupid—you know that. So smart, Gabriel
was, so *bright*—always. *(beat)* He must have
thought he was never going to fit here—and so he
made a DECISION. For the first time ever, Gabriel
put himself first. Do you see? He wasn't going to
play himself out for anyone—including us... All of
a sudden I understood everything in a different
way. See, for a second it was like I went into his
head—and I could see through his eyes—and feel
what he was feeling—I could, Ma. I could, I did.
I felt like I was almost jumping off into light—but
I came back again just as quick. I came back. Back
to reality—this FUCKING reality. And that's when
I realized the worst part of everything... he couldn't
come back no more. This ...was... irreversible.
(beat) He decided everything. I hated him for
that—I did, and it was *pure*. In that moment,
I hated him so much, that if I could have—I would
have wrapped my hands around his neck, and

squeezed the life right out of him, myself. *(pause)* That's it. That is my last confession, Ma. *(beat)* I ran out of the room. I slammed the door shut. I went to the phone in the upstairs hall and started dialing any phone number I knew. I called Pa at work, the police, his high school. I kept calling until I ran out of numbers. I have no clue what I said. *(beat)* When I was done, I went into the bathroom. I washed my face, and when I looked in the mirror—I saw that one of my eyes was completely filled with red; *blood*, something had burst. I pushed all his stuff off the counter. Razor, zit-cream, comb, toothbrush, gel, all of it—OUT! That's when I went and sat down on the weight-scale. That's what I did. That is *everything*. I sat on the weight-scale, and I waited for the screaming to start.

Lights shift slightly, as:

Scene Twenty-seven

PAOLO enters. He slowly walks all the way around the table before arriving at his seat. He takes a long inhale before he slowly sits. There is an eerie finality to his method. His seat is lit overhead by a harsh light. The light above him quickly grows to a high intensity—then:

Lights return to the earlier state as PAOLO will remain on stage for the rest of the play. He sits in his chair throughout the following scenes.

Scene Twenty-eight

MARCO and CONCETTA, in their last position on top of the table.

MARCO That's everything. I sat on the weight-scale, and I waited for the screaming to start.

MARCO looks down for a moment. He is spent, but hopeful. He wipes his face of everything, and looks up. He looks to his mother. She is already looking at him. Locked in a gaze that is impenetrable. Glassy-eyed. She no longer speaks in the present. She is floating above the reality of this moment.

CONCETTA There are things that you cannot take away from me.

MARCO –I'm not trying to take anything, Ma.

CONCETTA There is one reality that no one can change. I am a *mother*. Even after I am dead, I will still have died a mother.

MARCO –Mamma…?

CONCETTA I am still his mother—no one else can say that. Only me. I am the only one who knows what I went through to protect him inside me. All the little secrets a mother keeps to herself for fear she may tempt fate. The first time he moved in my stomach—like a little silver fish in a glass. So light, so gentle—just so much that I could feel his little tail brush against me, inside.

She makes a little fluttering move with her fingers to demonstrate.

(beat) Only I know the pain of feeling him push through my small hips, his poor little elbows pushing, pushing to make room—and me waiting to hear my bones snap inside me. I am the only one who remembers the moment when fear covered me like a wet blanket—my whole body shaking because he was not out yet. Him stuck, and me shaking crazy, like a horse. I know how I prayed to God to take, to lift that fear from me, and deliver my Gabriele safe. I pictured him inside trying so hard, and I convinced myself to stop the shaking, and I got him to move through me. Me, and God, and Gabriele. We are the only ones who *know* for sure what are miracles.

MARCO makes the sad realization that she is once again departed. Lost.

MARCO   *(gently)* Ma? Who are you talking to? *(beat) Please.* Talk to me. *I'm* right here.

> *She starts fixing her appearance—however the attempt is pathetic. She now speaks as though MARCO weren't there—speaking once again to her unseen sympathetic companion. She smiles, knowingly.*

CONCETTA   Everyone knows better than me how I should be. They come into my home like a terrible storm, and open up all the doors and the windows and the cupboards—but who told them they could do this to my home? Who said they could destroy everything that I am keeping safe? All they do is destroy, and it's always Concettina who has to sweep up what is left. I *am* a stupid woman—BUT, I understand one thing they don't. *(beat) (with frightening clarity)* How can you look for reality, when you are searching from inside of a *dream.* How? *(beat)* You cannot.

> *Pause. CONCETTA looks at the rosary in her hand. After a beat, she slowly puts the rosary around her neck like a necklace.*

This is just a bad dream, but he is still my boy. I keep everything ready for him; his clothes, his books, a bigger bed—so that he knows I never stopped to care… I never stopped protecting him. And when I finally do wake up from this nightmare, I will get out of my bed, walk down the hallway to his bedroom. I will open his door—and there he will be…

> *Silence. MARCO looks at his mother.*

MARCO   I have to go. I can't stay here. *(beat)* I can't be here no more.

> *He walks off the stage.*

> *After a beat. CONCETTA looks around and realizes for the first time that MARCO is gone.*

(l to r:) Paul Fauteux and Toni Ellwand, Buddies in Bad Times production, March, 2006. *photo by Dennis Horn*

CONCETTA I'm so cold. *(pause)* This house is frozen.

> *She leaves walking backwards, looking at the emptiness of her home the whole time.*
>
> *After she has left, without responding in any way to what has occurred, PAOLO very slowly turns in his chair, so that his back faces the audience, his hands are upturned in his lap, his shoulders weak, his head hangs low. He looks only at his hands.*
>
> *Cross into:*

Scene Twenty-nine

> *MATT stands at the front of a class. He is in the middle of his presentation on Gravity and the Universe, from the beginning of the play. The completed model of the solar system is set up before him on a desk. He is grief-stricken—trying to regain his composure. He is subdued. He refers to a paper.*

MATT Everything I just read, up until now, is what Gabriel wrote for the project—I mostly worked on the model part.

> *He clears his throat, folds the piece of paper, and speaks.*

Before I go, I just want to add something. With everything that happened this week, it's been really hard for everyone, I know. But, it's also made me start looking at things in a new way. So… Last night, I had a lot of trouble sleeping—I was… well, I ended up writing another conclusion to this presentation. I hope it makes sense to you. *(pause)* I did this project on the universe, but never once did I actually look up at the night sky. I learned about the sad truth of gravity here on Earth, but only when it affected me—it is true that everything that goes up, must come down… *(He tries to keep it together.)* There's so much going on all around us that we don't even notice—up there in space, there are asteroids hurtling through the silence, and from down here—we think they're beautiful… flashing across the sky. Most of us don't understand how brutal the whole process of a shooting star actually is, until it lands in your own living room.

> *Isolate CONCETTA standing on the bridge above the stage. We hear an unforgiving winter wind. We see very light snow falling. She is wearing her winter coat and boots, but it is unbuttoned and half off her shoulders. She wears Gabriel's rosary around her neck. She looks like a dangerous, empty ghost. Her body is shivering slightly, but she doesn't seem to notice. She is fixated on something on the horizon—an apparition. As it slowly unfolds, she feels a remarkable warmth grow inside her.*

(pause, as it finally dawns on him) Now I know. I finally understand why we don't look up: because, it takes huge courage. Because you may see things that will change you forever. And, understanding exactly how certain things work, can set you free, or it can shut you down forever. You want to know what I learned about the universe we live in? *(beat)* We have to *live* in it. We have to show up to our own life, otherwise it'll just happen to us. *(beat)* I learned that to create the desire in someone to grow, is really, really hard to do—but to *kill* that desire, is way too easy. *(beat)* That's what I learned. *(beat)* Question all of it. That's all.

> *CONCETTA lets her coat drop. CONCETTA slowly steps forward towards the edge. She is glowing.*

CONCETTA   *Faith. You see? (beat) Here I am. Waiting; my faith on my face.*

MATT   Now I *know.*

> *CONCETTA is right up against the railing. Her eyes follow the drop, then begin to trace back up towards the horizon of the night sky and then,*

finally, beyond it: She sees her son. CONCETTA quietly gasps:

CONCETTA ...Gabriele.

MATT takes in a deep breath, as if he has shaken off a huge weight. He looks up and out, to where he has placed his friend.

MATT *(beat)* Thank you.

We hear the sound of cars on a highway build to an uncomfortable level, before dropping out—leaving the sad, hopeful strain of the cello. An intense light illuminates CONCETTA, it spreads across the ceiling of light, filling the space. She is seeing something beautiful—direct correspondence. Her hands rise up to reach the apparition. She laughs and cries at the same time. After a few moments, her head slowly comes back down, as she brings her hands to her heart. Her face registers relief for the first time.

CONCETTA ...Grazie.

She smiles. Lights snap out on her. MATT is now facing ahead. He smiles.

MATT Thank you. *(beat)* Thanks.

Slowly, finally the last bulb which has been fading throughout, goes out. Darkness for a beat before: Every bulb in the ceiling of light glows like stars in a night sky, before slowly fading to blackout.

In Gabriel's Kitchen • 107

photo by Ian Brown

SALVATORE ANTONIO was born in Toronto, Canada, and trained as an actor at the prestigious National Theatre School of Canada, where he is now a guest instructor. Known primarily for his work on stage, screen and television, *In Gabriel's Kitchen* is his first full-length play. Since its premiere at Buddies in Bad Times Theatre in Toronto in March 2006, *In Gabriel's Kitchen* has been produced in Italian translation, at Teatro Della Limonaia in Florence, Italy, and is set to have its US premiere at The New Conservatory Theater of San Francisco in early 2008. As a writer, Salvatore has been Playwright-In-Residence at Buddies in Bad Times Theatre (Toronto), where he was also a member of the AnteChamber Writers' Unit. He is currently a member of the Writers' Unit at Tarragon Theatre (Toronto), where he is working on two new plays: *LOAD* and *The Coronation of Medusa Regina*.